Moses Was a Welshman

The (Mostly) True Stories of Two
Unforgettable West Wales Families

Kay McAnally & Andrea Sutcliffe

The authors would like to thank the Scolton Manor Museum, Haverfordwest, Wales, for permission to reprint the following Tom Mathias photos from its collection: pages 7; 8, left; 15, right; 21; 23; 25; 26; 32; 33; 36 top and bottom left; 63; 71; 73; 91; 103; 106. All other photographs are from the authors' personal collections.

Dolbadau Road Press

Front cover photo: Probably taken by Tom Mathias in the mid-1930's, this photo shows two great friends and cousins getting ready to go fishing in their coracles on the Teifi River below Cilgerran: Tom Griffiths (left) and John Moses Griffiths.

Back cover photo: Found in Nesta Griffiths's personal collection; the photographer, the people in the photo, and the location are unknown.

To our mothers, Nora (1926-2011)
and Nesta (1921-2008)

To storytellers everywhere—past, present and future—
who preserve family memories and give us roots

and

To Tom Mathias (1866-1940),
Whose photographs let us see our families' faces

Contents

Preface

It was Christmas Eve 2007. I hadn't seen my mother, Nora, so excited in a long time. My "Welsh" cousin Andrea Sutcliffe had sent Mom a Christmas letter full of family news from the past twenty years. We had lost touch with her family years earlier and hadn't been able to locate them. My mother feared she would never see her cousin, Nesta, Andrea's mother, ever again. But it turned out that Nesta was only a short drive away, Andrea wrote, and was not doing well. She wanted to see Nora.

Mom shoved the phone in my hand as I walked through her door with my arms loaded with gifts. She said, "Let's phone her right now! Right this minute! I want to see Nesta!" She didn't care about any gift other than the one at the end of the phone line.

A week later, we made the drive from Austin to San Antonio. The trip provided Mom with a perfect opportunity to make sure that I had remembered the family's stories from Cilgerran, Wales. (I had them memorized after sixty years of hearing them!) "Just in case," though, she told them to me again…and again. She never tired of them and could hardly wait to have another opportunity to recall them with the very person who had experienced many of them with her: Nesta.

When the two cousins saw each other again after so many years, the energy in the room was palpable. I phoned Andrea and placed my cell phone on the table between our two mothers so she could hear their laughter and the re-telling of their stories too. I decided there and then that I would research the Griffiths family tree for Mom.

Before I could finish my thoughts, Nesta told Mom that Andrea had been researching the Griffiths family. I retrieved my phone from the table (they never even noticed it was there) to ask her about any progress with her genealogy efforts. We decided to work on the project together, via emails. As soon as I got home and on my computer, I started looking….

What a bewildering array! All those Cilgerran Griffithses (in particular all those men named Moses) and Evanses and Thomases and…who was who? They were all just names on records. None of them was recognizable and none of them seemed "real." If I showed Mom a family tree full of those names, she wouldn't understand it any more than I did. Stories are what had painted pictures of Mom's family—she could see them. Names on records didn't say a thing.

Serendipity took over. Through an odd combination of strange coincidences and happy encounters, Andrea and I found ourselves matching photographs that her great-grandfather Tom Mathias had taken to some of the names on the Griffiths side of the family. Some of the photos also identified the places that were in our mothers' stories. After months of discovery we finally had a family tree with names, faces, stories and places—and relatives we could relate to. Our family history was beginning to make sense.

It is my hope that the family stories Andrea and I have re-told here will help to reveal the very human people whose lives had been reduced to brief entries on a family tree. But I hope they do even more. My wish is that they will inspire readers to appreciate the unique gift of their own family stories, and to dig deeper into their roots, to discover, like we have, the people who have made us who we are. —*Kay McAnally*

Introduction

This all began with a simple question about Moses Griffiths. "Mom," I asked the former Nesta Griffiths of Cilgerran, Wales, "I just learned that a fellow named Moses Griffiths lived around the corner from your house on Dolbadau Road. Were you related to him?"

"Oh, no, those Griffiths were no relation of ours!" she said with a scowl. I dropped the subject. (It turned out they were.)

But the puzzle presented by my initial look into Griffiths family history seemed to demand an answer. And what it led to—besides a confusing array of Cilgerran residents named Moses Griffiths— was a journey back to Wales and to the family I barely knew.

A few months earlier, I had decided it was time to learn more about my mother's relatives in Wales: the Mathias and Griffiths families of Cilgerran, on the Pembrokeshire and Cardiganshire border. The only ones I had known personally, mostly via those flimsy blue aerogram letters from across the Atlantic—were my grandmother, Frances Matilda Mathias Griffiths (Tilla); my great-grandmother, Louise Paquier Mathias, and great-uncle, James Mathias; a great-aunt, May Griffiths; and Nora, Kay, and Christianne, my Griffiths cousins in Austin, Texas.

I thought this project would please my mother, then eighty years old, but I was wrong. Whether it was her growing memory loss or her deepening depression over my father's recent death, she was just not that interested. I did a little research, hit some dead-ends, and went on to other things.

A few years later, Nesta began her downhill slide into dementia, just as her mother had two decades earlier. She knew what was happening and seemed to face it bravely, if sadly. She began telling me more stories about her life in Wales, and reciting poetry and singing songs in Welsh. These activities seemed to make her happier than she had been in a long time. Her sentimental journey to the past gave me an idea. I would try to locate her Welsh cousin in the States and arrange for a reunion.

Nesta and her cousin, Nora, were Griffiths girls who had grown up together in Cilgerran. They both had married American GIs after the end of WWII and both had moved to Texas. This was a lucky coincidence for both of them, for these two undoubtedly homesick young women started their new American lives only an hour's drive apart.

There were many visits back and forth between our homes in San Antonio and Austin in the 1950's and early 1960's, and my sister, Marcia, and I loved playing with our cousins Kay and Chris.

But by the 1980's, events had conspired to disconnect the two families, and Nora's remarriage and my parents' moves made it difficult for them to find each other years later. For once, the Internet was no help in my search, mostly because I wasn't sure of Nora's married name or even if she was still alive. Every few months I would enter in the name and address I found in an old address book of my mother's, but I always came up with nothing.

One day in December of 2007, after returning to my home in Virginia from a trip to see my mother, something told me to try again. That time it worked, but in a rather bizarre way. Nora's name and town came up in the obituary of a woman who had recently died near Austin. I searched the Internet for that name and town and found an address. That day I mailed a Christmas letter to her. On Christmas night the phone rang, and Kay was on the line. Nora was fine—Kay was visiting for Christmas—and we talked excitedly for an hour trying to catch up on thirty years of two very different lives. A week later, Kay took Nora to my mother's nursing home in San Antonio, as Kay recounts in the preface to this book.

My mother died a month later. Kay and Nora returned for her memorial service, where Nora regaled the guests with stories of two long-ago Welsh childhoods.

Later, Marcia and I packed up her few remaining possessions. Included were bags and boxes of old photos. Luckily for all of us, Marcia had asked our mother about many of the pictures during her visits and had written names and dates on the backs of many of them. (Lesson to families everywhere: make sure you write names, dates and places on the backs of all of your photos—or in the online caption. Your descendants will thank you.) Little did we realize then how valuable those photos would become to us a few years later. My interest in learning more about our mother's family returned, now that I had rediscovered Kay and Nora.

Kay also began trying to sort out the Griffiths family. She had discovered that we had Griffiths ancestors on two sides, going way back (to the first Moses Griffiths (b. 1781), whom we soon nicknamed "Big Daddy" Moses, to identify him as the source of all the other Moseses) as well as some Thomases and Evanses. When my husband, Ed, and I had traveled to Wales in 2005, we explored cemeteries in and around Cilgerran in search of more details.

In the fall of 2008, several months after my mother died, we returned to Wales, this time meeting up with Kay at our cottage rental outside Cardigan. She lugged around a huge binder full of her research, and we again risked twisted ankles traipsing through muddy cemeteries, trying hard to read faded headstones inscribed in Welsh. One day we even made a trip in a drenching rain up to the National Library in Aberystwyth to look at old parish records. We made minor progress.

Then Nora died in June 2011, just a month after our second trip with Kay to Wales. Nora's mind was sharp to the end, and the last time I saw her, in an Austin hospital, she was having a ball, entertaining me (and the nursing staff) with hilarious yarns about Wales and Cilgerran and the Griffiths family. As Kay says, Nora was blessed with the Welsh gift of *hwyl*.

It had long been in our minds to try to preserve these stories in some way, but everyday life took over for a while. Then one day in late 2012, while Kay was searching the Internet for a photo of her great-grandfather that Tom Mathias had taken of him, she came across a young woman in Cardiff named Angharad Evans. As we were soon to learn, Angharad had grown up in my great-grandfather's house in Cilgerran and was a teacher and a member of the National Theater of Wales. One of her planned experimental theater projects had to do with Tom Mathias and his subjects.

Kay and I offered to help, and we began sending her our write-ups of the stories our mothers had told us about life in Cilgerran. These stories would, we hoped, illuminate the long-ago lives of the people in Tom's photographs.

Since the late 1980's, Tom Mathias's 500 or so glass-plate photographs from the early twentieth century have formed a collection curated by Mark Thomas at Scolton Manor, the Pembrokeshire County Museum. It all began in the late 1970's, when Angharad's father, William Evans, bought the Mathias property after the death of my great-uncle James. He soon began discovering stacks of decades-old glass photographic plates in the farm's outbuildings.

As luck would have it, a retired Royal Air Force photographer named Max Davis had recently moved to Boncath, near Cilgerran. One evening William ran into him at a local pub and told him about the plates. Max and his wife, Peggy, soon set upon the task of making prints from plates that were relatively undamaged and then trying to identify—with the help of local newspapers—the people in the pictures. Several local exhibits followed in the 1980's, and my mother and father attended at least one of these and became friends with Max and Peggy.

Oddly, just two days after our first contact with Angharad, we discovered that Theatre Mwldan in Cardigan had opened an exhibit featuring Tom Mathias's photos. A new generation would now be seeing his century-old images.

All of this renewed interest in Tom Mathias set us to start going through old family photographs. To our great surprise, we found many more of his photos, but taken with more modern cameras in the 1920's and 1930's. Figuring out who was who became great sport as scanned images flew back and forth in emails among Marcia in Washington State, Kay in Texas, and me in Virginia.

We began to get the feeling that our ancestors in Cilgerran were somehow conspiring to make this project happen. "Remember us" they seemed to say, "Don't forget the lives we lived and the times we spent in this sometimes harsh but always beautiful place." The stories of the Mathias and Griffiths families that follow have their roots in our mothers' memories, but we wrote them ourselves, sometimes using first person in an attempt to personalize their accounts. Although the stories may not be completely accurate in certain minor details (where we were obliged to fill in gaps using our best guesses), they are certainly mostly true, both in fact and in spirit.

Angharad once asked me why I was so drawn to Wales, why I kept coming back. I replied that there was something almost mystical about the pull it had on me, the way it made me feel when I was there. It felt like home, even though I had no right to call it home. When I talked with Kay and Marcia about this, they said they felt the same way. Later we learned there is a Welsh word for that feeling: *hiraeth*. It has no direct English translation but conveys, in part, a sense of a longing for something that can never be yours.

That word describes our feelings perfectly. —*Andrea Sutcliffe*

The authors' mothers, cousins Nora Larsen and Nesta Griffiths, Cilgerran, 1935 (Tom Mathias)

Aberdyfan, with members of the Tom Mathias family, c. 1914 (Tom Mathias)

Home

Aberdyfan

The first time I saw Aberdyfan I was twelve years old. My Welsh-born mother, Nesta, had brought me and my sister from Texas to Cilgerran in the summer of 1961 so we could meet and get to know our grandmother, Tilla, and our great-grandmother, Louise. Just as in the photo Tom Mathias had taken many years earlier, the old stone house was still in danger of being suffocated by some sort of vine.

We had been staying with my grandmother at Teifi View for a few days when finally the sun came out and it was time for the mile-long walk to Aberdyfan, on the outskirts of Cilgerran in the hamlet of Pontrhydyceirt. This was the house where my great-grandmother and her bachelor son, James, lived. Great-grandma's name was Louise Alice Paquier Mathias. Like my mother, she was an immigrant, except that she came to Wales rather than left it. Born in a perfect little village above Lake Geneva, the lithe and lovely Louise came to work as a governess at Castle Malgwyn, up the road in Llechryd, when she was in her early twenties. It was there she met Tom Mathias in the mid-1890's.

My mother told us all of this, I am sure, as we—along with my sister and our grandmother—set off in our Sunday best for Aberdyfan that summer day in 1961. I was not prepared for what I saw when we entered the dark house. Louise was dressed in black from head to toe. She was tiny—even I was taller—and she was very, very old. I had never seen anyone that old. We sat in her kitchen and sipped hot tea sweetened with honey. I had a hard time understanding her, but she seemed quite nice and happy to see us.

In 1870, Tom Mathias's father, James, bought Aberdyfan and several surrounding acres, known as Llwyncelyn, with a mortgage. He was twenty-nine years old, and Tom, his middle child, was four. It is not known where James and his wife, Frances, lived before Aberdyfan—perhaps with his parents, as was often the case in those hardscrabble days in Cilgerran. James was not a homebody: he was a ship's mate from the time he was a teenager. Records show that over the years he sailed to many exotic ports in Africa, the Mediterranean, the Azores, and the Americas.

Tom Mathias as a young man, 1890's; Louise Paquier, in London, c. 1895

8

Marcia, Tilla, and Andrea, on their way to Aberdyfan (seen in the distance), 1961

Sadly, Tom's mother, Frances, died just four years after James bought Aberdyfan. James remarried not long after, a young woman named Elizabeth, and she took care of his three children while he was away. He was home often enough, though, for they soon had a baby daughter, in 1879. But in 1884, James disappeared at sea, leaving Elizabeth penniless and with a newborn son. By then, Tom was eighteen and found a job with an insurance company in Cardigan to help pay the bills.

When Louise married Tom in 1896, she left her governess position at Castle Malgwyn and moved to Aberdyfan, squeezing herself into her new family—her mother-in-law and Tom's two half-siblings, Lizzie and Johnny. Louise and Tom's first child, Frances Matilda ("Tilla"), was born less than two years later, and their son, James, came along four years after that, in 1902. Louise spent the rest of her life in Aberdyfan, never returning to Switzerland. She had found a home in Wales, but that didn't keep her from longing for her childhood home in the Swiss vineyards, my mother often told me.

It was at Aberdyfan that Tom Mathias took up photography and turned it into a career. My mother said he was always more of a dreamer than a farmer. In going through his papers, I found proof of that: a packet of dunning notices that a Cardigan insurance company sent to Aberdyfan in the early 1900's. Of course, he may have just been short of funds at the time.

And it was at Aberdyfan, in the late 1970's, that its first new owner in more than a century discovered hundreds of Tom's old photographic plates stashed in outbuildings hither and yon, and recognized their value. Thank you, William Evans. —*AJS*

Teifi View with members of the Titus Griffiths family, c. 1914 (Tom Mathias)

Home

Teifi View

The Griffiths family home on Dolbadau Road in Cilgerran, called Teifi (or Tivy) View for more than a century (it was Penrhyw before that), is a simple Welsh cottage. Three windows up, three windows down, two front doors, three chimneys, and of course a slate roof. A noticeable change in the stonework at the rear of the house reveals that the second floor was added later to the original structure. A photograph taken by my great-grandfather, Tom Mathias, in 1914—with several Griffiths family members standing out front—shows the house seventy-five or eighty years after it was built. (He surely had no idea that a few years later, his sixteen-year-old daughter would marry the Griffiths lad standing in the doorway.)

Dolbadau Road connects Cilgerran's High Street with the Teifi River banks. Griffithses, many of them named Moses, appear to have lived on this short lane since at least the early 1800's. The village itself is ancient. Two of the village pubs, both still going strong, claim they've been serving brew here since the 1400's.

Cilgerran sits on the Pembrokeshire side of the River Teifi, just three miles from Cardigan. It was first mentioned by name in 1166. Six decades before that, the Normans had built a fort on a high cliff above the river, where today's castle ruins sit. But even earlier, some-one erected the Ogham stone that still stands in the St. Llawdogg's churchyard, proving that Irish people were living in the area by the 600's. Well before then, Iron Age residents built promontory forts nearby.

The year of Teifi View's construction is not known. My mother was told it was built in the 1830's, but that may have been the time of its enlargement. Sometime after the picture was taken, the far right door and two small windows were changed to match the others, and the front of the house was covered with rough-cast.

The last Griffiths to live there was Tilla Mathias Griffiths, who died at the age of ninety-two in 1990. Nesta, my mother, Tilla's only child, was born there in 1921. Nesta recalls Tilla saying that she loved the house as a child and dreamed of living there someday.

Tilla was a homebody of the first order. The only time she ever spent the night elsewhere, other than Aberdyfan, was when she was coaxed and cajoled into coming to her daughter's wedding in Cardiff in 1945. This was a woman who liked her own bed.

You could hardly blame her for not wanting to leave. The house, backed up against the side of a hill and sitting on the turn of the road, has a lovely view of the forests above the Teifi River, and presumably the Teifi itself in winter months (I have visited only in the other seasons). It is an easy, if uphill, walk to the High Street shops. Though Tilla lived alone there for most of her life (her first husband died young, and her second husband passed away just a few years into their marriage), she never lacked for company, and friends and neighbors were always dropping by. For nearly twenty years, she rearranged the furniture in her two downstairs rooms every Friday morning to accommodate the visiting doctor for the town surgery. On nice days she would take a book or her knitting outside and sit on the low stone wall across the road and chat with visitors walking down to the river.

Inside, the house was decidedly cozy. It would have been exceedingly cozy in the late 1890's, when ten people, mostly Griffiths children (including my recently born grandfather), were living in its three bedrooms and two sitting rooms. When I first saw it, as a child in 1961, I thought it was the most wonderful house I had ever seen. The front sitting room was tiny but inviting, with two overstuffed chintz-covered chairs flanking the fireplace. A fireplace! Living in a 1950's south Texas house, I did not know fireplaces.

As my younger sister, Marcia, and I explored the house—we were thrilled beyond belief to see there was an upstairs, another exotic feature—we noticed one disconcerting absence: a bathroom. Our mother took us outside and pointed to a small shed attached to the left side of the house, in the side garden. Oh. She opened the door and showed us the toilet, with the tank suspended high above. Just pull down the chain when you're through, she advised. Our next question was, What if we had to go in the middle of the night? (Who knew what was lurking in the dense woods nearby?) Not a problem, Mom said, and took us back upstairs to our bedroom and pulled a chamber pot out from under the bed. Use this, she said. We were speechless. I cried myself to sleep that night, not sure I would like this foreign country stuff. My tomboy sister, though, seemed fine with it, especially the lack of a bathtub.

Teifi View's location near the river, the woods, and Cilgerran Castle quickly overshadowed plumbing issues. Marcia and I had never, ever seen such greenery, such tall trees, and such a big river! It was late May, and the profusion of leafing trees and blooming shrubs and wildflowers, especially those amazing foxgloves, filled us with joy. We had read children's books by Enid Blyton for years—Grandma Tilla had posted them to us regularly—and now we felt we were living the stories.

Surely the villagers must have been peeking through their lace curtains and tsk-tsking at Nesta's two American ragamuffins who spent their days roaming the village and the surrounding woods, recreating the adventures of the Famous Five.

My mother, however, would have had a different take on Teifi View when she brought us there in 1961. This was Home. She had not seen it since the summer of 1947. The house probably hadn't changed much in those fourteen years, but surely her mother, now sixty-three years old, had. Their reunion was so tearful that my sister and I were denied entrance. Instead, we were entertained by a neighbor's daughter until it was deemed safe for us to go in.

Back in Texas, my mother would always be saying things like "Oh, I got a letter from home today," or "When I was home last," or "When we go home again in May." Home was always Cilgerran, always Teifi View. As kids, my sister and I often wondered how she referred to our house when she was away from it. We never figured it out, but we knew one thing for certain: the answer would not be "home." There was only one Home.

Years later, we figured it out. Home meant the place where her mother lived. When Tilla died, Nesta never went home again. She said she just couldn't. —*AJS*

Teifi View, late 1940's

14

Louise Paquier, 1896, the photo that started it all, taken by Tom Mathias on their first meeting; Tom Mathias self-portrait, early 1900's (both Tom Mathias)

Family

Mathias

One nice thing about doing genealogy research is that you get to know about family members without ever having to actually put up with them. Of course, there are exceptions—for example, I wish I could have back the hours with my Welsh grandmother that I squandered long ago—but on the whole, having certain relatives on paper rather than snoring on your sofa is probably a good thing.

The challenges of researching family history in Wales have been daunting. Just as in the opening scene of an old Hugh Grant movie, which shows someone searching through a Welsh phone directory ("…there is an extraordinary shortage of last names in Wales"), my cousin Kay and I soon realized that there were a lot of Griffithses in Cilgerran, many of them with the same first names. Our mothers were not much help in sorting them out; they denied kinship with the ones they didn't know or like, even though further research usually proved them wrong. It seems that some of our ancestors must have stepped out for air (or were hiding in the attic) when the census-taker came round, for there are a few family members who remain unaccounted for in certain years, even though we are sure they were living in Cilgerran at the time.

Many of our relatives also failed to register births and deaths with the county. However, they apparently could not escape marriage registration, which has revealed some pretty eye-popping facts. Kay and I discovered that we each have a close female ancestor whose first-born child arrived a little too soon—one of them a whole year before the wedding, one just a few months after. We have wondered, in that era of no privacy at home, did conception take place in some nook or cranny of Cilgerran Castle, or perhaps deep in the woods next to the river? We will never know, but the thought of it makes our relatives seem like a lot more fun—and a lot more human.

One can't help but wonder what traits and temperaments we have inherited from our ancestors. Luckily, we seem to have avoided debilitating hereditary diseases and tendencies toward madness, although the jury is still out on a fondness for alcohol. We have several relatives (mostly women) who lived into their nineties—Aunty May was ninety-nine!—and those who died too young (mostly men).

The desire of our family members to move away from home, or the need to stay put, is a more common thread. On the Griffiths side over the past century, more left Cilgerran than stayed—in fact, all six female children of Titus Griffiths and Martha Evans Griffiths left, while the two males stayed. But between the 1780's and 1900's, so far as we can tell, the farthest any Griffiths or Thomas or Evans had ever moved was between Llechryd and Cilgerran.

On the Mathias side, we have a mix of movers and stayers. James Mathias, who died in a bizarre event at sea, left Cilgerran as a teenager to become a mariner; but his son, Tom, the photographer, never left his little corner of Cilgerran. Tom's daughter, Tilla, was a stayer of the first order, but her daughter, Nesta (a Griffiths-Mathias), moved bravely across the Atlantic; both her daughters are also movers, but with a homebody gene or two.

Nora (a Griffiths-Larsen), also moved to America, where one daughter is a mover and one a stayer. Nora's brother Willie spent most of his life as a teacher in Tasmania—just about as far away as you can get from Cilgerran. Nora's other brother, Kai, stayed in Great Britain.

Those of us on the Mathias side like to think, mostly without good cause, that we have inherited Tom Mathias's photographic eye. We all love photography; Tom's great-great-granddaughter, Stephanie, has even sold some of her work professionally. We also agree that the love of nature that Tom instilled in his granddaughter, Nesta, successfully carried through to his great-grandchildren and great-great-grandchildren.

Perhaps none of those traits means a thing, genetically. We are all shaped by many other things from the time we are small. But knowing something about our ancestors can help us understand our place in the grand scheme of things, and perhaps a little bit of why we are who we are.

When we can see—through Tom's photos—our families' faces, the places where they lived and worked, and learn more about the times they lived in, then perhaps that knowledge will give us pause, and make us grateful. –*AJS*

Tom's Story

A Life Behind the Camera

I was born in the ancient village of Cilgerran, near where Cardiganshire meets Pembrokeshire, in West Wales. The year of my birth was 1866. People had already been living there for a long time when the Normans built a castle above the Teifi River in the 1200's.

My father, James Mathias, was a ship's mate who had grown up in Cilgerran; his father had been born there, too. James was often at sea. My two sisters—one a year younger, one a year older—and I did our best to help our mother run the farm while he was away. In 1870, my father had bought a farm and two small cottages known as Aberdyfan and Ty-y-bont, on the outskirts of Cilgerran. He enlarged Aberdyfan to two stories so that my grandmother and two aunts could live with us.

Just four years later, when I was eight years old, my mother died. Some time after that my father married a young girl named

Elizabeth from the village, and fairly soon after that another sister came along.

When I was eighteen, in the late summer of 1884, we received terrible news. A letter arrived saying that my father had disappeared at sea. Gone, just like that. No bodies were ever found. The ship he was on—a small sailing brig—had delivered a load of salt to a port near Labrador, Newfoundland, and was heading to another port to pick up a load of fish. No one has ever figured out what happened. On a calm, clear day in August, the ship—its name was Resolven, after the town near Neath—was found drifting off the coast. Not a soul was on board, but there was food on the table, and the stove fire was burning. The small tender boat was missing. Back home in Cilgerran, my little brother, Johnny, had just been born.

Our family fell apart at this horrible news. I eventually found a job in Cardigan selling insurance. Cardigan was a very busy place in those days, but it was nearing the end of its days as an important shipping port. With my salary and the money we made by selling eggs and honey from our farm, we kept our family going. Really, our troubles were not much different from our neighbors, and at least we were healthy.

Growing up, I was a curious lad. I would devour any books or newspapers I could find. I especially loved nature—the stars in the sky, the plants and animals around our farm, all held an endless fascination for me. I tried to learn everything about them.

But what changed my life was photography. I will always remember when I first knew about cameras. It was while I was working in Cardigan that I met a fellow named Allen who had a photography studio on Priory Street. I pestered the poor man with questions about cameras and how they worked and how he developed the pictures. I learned a lot from him, but most of all he taught me how to use a camera and how to develop the plates in a darkroom. For a long time I saved what money I could and finally was able to buy one of his old cameras. I used his darkroom until I could build one of my own at Aberdyfan.

I began to help Mr. Allen with his business. When I learned enough—and I must say I was a pretty quick study—he would send me out to take Sunday school class pictures, things like that. It wasn't easy getting twenty or thirty people lined up and making them stand perfectly still while I fiddled with the camera and changed the plates. But I enjoyed doing it and was able to make a little extra money.

In a few years I was able to set up my own business as a photographer. One day Mr. Gower of Castle Malgwyn up the road in Llechryd—that was one of those huge stone mansions the rich English gentry built with all the money they made from our slate quarries here—well, he asked me to take pictures of his family. He had several small children, and they had a governess who spoke French and a little English, which I guess was good because the English gentry wanted their children to learn French.

The governess's name was Louise Paquier. She was perhaps twenty-two years old, a tiny wisp of a girl. Later someone told me she had come all the way from Switzerland with her sister to find work. When I tried to talk to her in Welsh, she didn't understand me, and she said something back in French, which of course I didn't understand at all. But we each knew some English, so that was how we talked to each other. We laughed, and I took pictures of the children and left. But I could not forget her sweet smile. I returned a few days later to take more photographs and perhaps—I hoped—to see her again. —*AJS*

Castle Malgwyn, Llechryd, early 1900's (Tom Mathias)

Louise and Tilla, 1900 (Tom Mathias)

Louise's Story

A Swiss Girl Far from Home

I will tell you the story of how I came to live in Wales. I was born in the pretty little village of Bursins, a couple of miles above the town of Rolle on the shores of Lake Geneva, Switzerland, in 1872. My family had vineyards on the hillsides near our house and grew grapes for the local wineries. I could look out my upstairs bedroom window and see all the way to the blue waters of the lake in the distance. For as long as I lived, I would always remember that beautiful place.

In those days, if a girl wasn't married by the time she was in her early twenties, it was time for her to look for work. Our village was small and our parents had little money, so my sister and I decided to be adventurous and leave Switzerland. We thought we could find

23

jobs as governesses and travel the world. It all sounded so exciting. For some reason that I can no longer recall, I ended up in a very remote area of West Wales, while my sister found a job in Greece. She had better weather, but I found a nice English family to employ me, the Gowers, and I grew to love their children.

But my life there was quite lonely. I didn't quite fit in with the Welsh servants, and wasn't really part of the family. I became quite homesick. I often thought of going home, but I was so horribly seasick on the voyage over that I knew I would never get on a ship again.

One day a young man came to take pictures of the Gower children. He was rather good-looking and was a little quiet and shy, and very polite. A few weeks later, I saw him at the chapel in Llechryd. After Sunday school, he came over to talk to me, and after that we courted for a few months. He was the most religious man I had ever known, and that was very important to me, to find a good and decent man.

By 1896 we were married. I left my job at Castle Malgwyn and moved into Aberdyfan with Tom and his family. The house may not seem very large when you look at it today, but compared to most of the farmhouses in our area it seemed quite grand to me.

Two years later, I gave birth to our first child, a girl we named after Tom's mother and my mother: Frances Matilda. Four years later, we had a boy, whom we named James Henry, after Tom's father and my father. That was how you named your children in those days. People would be shocked if you didn't!

The children and the house and the farm kept me very busy, but in all those years I never got over my homesickness for Switzerland. I never saw my parents again. We had no money for such a trip, and even if we had, I couldn't stand the thought of being seasick again. In fact, I never traveled any farther than Cardigan for the rest of my life.

Some of my happiest days were when my sister and her daughters would come to visit. By then, my sister had married well and was living in London. My lovely nieces—Paulette and Helene—came to Cilgerran for visits for the rest of my life.

Tilla Mathias, c. 1910 (Tom Mathias)

Our daughter—we called her Tilla, short for Matilda—was very strong-headed. Like so many mothers and daughters, we often did not get along. She refused to go to chapel and could be quite sulky.

I must say I was almost glad to see her get married and move into her husband's family home on Dolbadau Road. She had been seeing a boy named Tommy Griffiths from the village. His older brother owned one of the slate quarries along the river. Tom was not in favor of the courtship and tried to discourage it. But Tilla was always headstrong, and one day she announced she was with child.

What could we do? This sort of thing happened more than you would think, but that didn't make it any easier for us. A few months later Nesta was born. They named her after the legendary Princess Nest of Cilgerran Castle.

James Mathias feeding a robin, c. 1910 (Tom Mathias)

Our son, James, still lived at home with us, and he was such a good lad. He was sweet and bright and gentle from the day he was born. He was such help to his father in running the farm, and he also helped me with the household chores after Tilla moved out.

I am afraid I did a bad thing regarding James, though. I wouldn't let him get married. This was many years later—he must have been thirty years old. He came to me in the kitchen one morning as I was having my tea and seemed quite nervous. Finally, he worked up the courage to tell me he had met a nice girl and wanted to marry her. I am afraid I didn't hesitate. I told him absolutely that he could not, that I would not allow it. I told him his duty as a son was to take care of me and his father. Tom was not always in good health, and James took care of so many things for us. We could have hardly survived without him during those terrible Depression years. He sadly obeyed my wishes.

Tom died in 1940, but I lived for another twenty-six years, with my dear boy James by my side the whole time. He was such a comfort to me. My daughter, Tilla, would visit even more often as I grew older and would cook and do laundry for me. It was such a blessing to have those two good children. —*AJS*

James Mathias, early 1920's (both by Tom Mathias)

Tilla with Nesta, 1922 (Tom Mathias)

Tilla's Story

Cilgerran's Good Neighbor

I adored my father, Tom Mathias. He and I were the closest of all the fathers and daughters I knew. He was so interested in everything around him, and luckily he passed that love of knowledge on to me.

My mother and I, on the other hand, were always at odds. But as I grew older, I realized she had led a hard and often unhappy life, so different from the one she must have imagined for herself when she left Switzerland. At least she could depend on my brother—he was always so devoted to her.

It is interesting, how we see things when we are young, and then we learn too late how wrong we were. I could not wait to leave my home at Aberdyfan when I was a girl. I wanted to get away from my mother's grip and have my own family. I had known Tommy Griffiths for as long as I could remember. We were the same age and went to the same school. He was the youngest child in a large family—he had a much older brother, by nineteen years—William—and six older sisters—Hannah, Myfawny, Maria, Margaret, Louisa, and Mary Ann. William owned one of the quarries on the river and did very well; his sisters all eventually married and moved away. Tommy, being the youngest, lived with his mother at Teifi View. His father, Titus, had died when Tommy was only four years old.

I have to tell you that as a girl I always loved that house, Teifi View. I would pass it when I walked down from High Street to the river, or when I was walking up to Cilgerran from the river path from Llechryd. I was strangely drawn to it.

After our schooling ended—I guess I was about sixteen—I got a job in Cardigan in a milliner's shop, helping to make hats. It is hard to imagine now, but in those days ladies' hats were very important. There were five or six milliners in Cardigan, and they were always looking for girls who had skillful hands to help them. The little bit of money I made helped my parents pay the bills.

I never really courted anyone but Tommy Griffiths. We began to see each other and go for walks in the countryside around Cilgerran. He was working in his brother's slate quarry workshop at the far end of High Street, not too far from my home, Aberdyfan, learning how to split the slate to make roofing tiles. He became quite good at it.

Tommy hated the hard labor of working with the slate. He wanted to go to school to learn engineering. He had taught himself how to repair clocks and other types of machinery and was very good at it. But his brother said no, that he must stay with the family business, and that there was no money for fancy schools. And that was that. The problem was that Tommy was too good at what he did, and William could not afford to lose his skills.

30

Tom Griffiths, c. 1918, Cardigan

Our marriage happened shortly after I realized I was pregnant. When our baby, a precious little girl we named Nesta, was born in January 1921, I was living with Tommy and his mother, Martha, in Teifi View.

Sometimes Martha would go up to High Street and live for a while with her older son, William, in the house called Lyndhurst. That would give me and Tommy a break. But as she got older and became more forgetful and confused, she lived much of the time with us, and I would look after her. It was her house, after all. She died in 1931, when Nesta was ten years old.

Every summer, my husband's niece Sarah Mary would bring her family back to Cilgerran. They would stay with her father at Lyndhurst. But it seems the children—Willie, Kai, and little Nora—were always at our house, playing with their cousin Nesta.

One day I heard screams coming from the garden, and I ran out to find that Willie had pushed Nora, who was about four at the

31

time, down the hill into a bed of nettles. Poor child, I carried her inside and covered her with calamine lotion.

The three children loved to sing along when Nesta played the piano—she was self-taught and quite good at it. Every Sunday, the News of the World newspaper printed sheet music, so the children always had new songs to learn. I remember their favorite was "Up a Lazy River."

Tommy's job at his uncle's quarry workshop meant that he was around slate dust all day long. His lungs must have been filled with the stuff, for he developed asthma so severe that he had trouble breathing. His coughing just grew worse and worse. In those days, there were no medicines for asthmatics—and not a thing any doctor could do.

In 1938, when he was barely forty years old, we lost him. Nesta was seventeen and had just been accepted to nursing school. I would soon be all alone. —*AJS*

Dolbadau Quarry workshop, Cilgerran, 1920's (Tom Mathias)

Nesta Griffiths, 1922 (Tom Mathias)

Nesta's Story

I Met My Fate That Night

I couldn't see how I could leave my mother all alone in that house. We had both been torn to pieces by my father's death. He was a dear man and the best of fathers. I seriously thought about staying home with my mother in Cilgerran and not going nursing school. I could have learned typing and stenography and probably found a job in an office in Cardigan. But the idea of being cooped up all day in a boring office did not appeal to me.

My mother insisted I go and get on with my life, and so quite reluctantly I did. When I came home on breaks from school, she seemed to be doing okay, even though there wasn't much money. She was always a strong and independent woman, and a very kind one, and everyone in the village loved her and wanted to help her. And she was always there to help them.

It was good that she was living close to her parents as they got older. Her father, Tom Mathias, was by then in his seventies and not in the best of health, and she now had time to help her mother and James take care of things on the farm and around the house.

Speaking of my grandfather, I hold dear, fond memories of him. He doted on me, being his only grandchild, and we were quite close. He was a religious man, a man of high principles, always honest and sincere. [*The following eight paragraphs are memories Nesta wrote and shared with Max Davis when the Mathias photos were first exhibited in the 1980's.*]

He was a self-taught man and was interested in everything around him, especially astronomy, birds, plants, flowers, and so on. He also loved to teach. I used to visit my grandparents quite often as a child—they lived about a mile away. My grandfather would take me for walks and stop to pick out a flower, explain how it grew, and name all its different segments.

He thought it would be good for me to have a small garden of my own. So he set aside a flowerbed for me—it was for me to plant and take care of year around. That lasted a couple of years, and I was quite proud of it. It was quite a thrill watching things grow.

At night when the stars were bright he would bring out his telescope and point out and name the planets, galaxies, and stars.

He also took up painting and tried to teach me. I remember him explaining how to make the hills of mountains in the background appear to be far away and how to mix the colors.

He was a very enthusiastic beekeeper and knew everything there was to know about bees. I was stung more than once when the time came to take the honey or when there was a swarm of bees that he would be smoking out of the apple trees. I also remember him being quite proud of himself for developing an apple that would keep well during the winter months.

Nesta at bridge over the Dyfan (Tom Mathias)

Most of all he loved photography. If it was a nice day, out would come the camera. He would pick out the background very carefully. I remember one he took of me standing on a little wooden bridge he had built over the small stream—the Dyfan—that ran through one of the fields he called the meadow. He would wait patiently for the right light, going back several times to look through the camera with the black cloak over his head. To me it seemed like an eternity and I would get very restless before he finally took the picture. I still remember the first time he showed me how he developed a picture—seeing it slowly coming into view as he gently moved the tray containing the solution. It seemed like magic to me then.

One of the last memories I have of him was during haymaking time. That was when neighboring farmers came to help. The work was hard and long, but as children we thought it was a picnic. How we loved to slide down the haystacks—and we would get told off for it, too! Nothing tasted better than those sandwiches and ginger beer for lunch and at tea time the cake and the hot tea from a big aluminum jug. But as we grew older and had to pitch in, we realized it was hard work.

Lunch break during haymaking at Aberdyfan; Louise, left, Tilla, right (Tom Mathias)

Tilla and Nesta, 1938; Tom Griffiths, 1930's, Cilgerran (probably by Tom Mathias)

He died in 1940, less than two years after my father died. All this great loss within such a short time was quite hard for me and my mother and my grandmother.

To make matters worse, by then I was working at a hospital in Cardiff, and Britain was at war with Germany. It was such a terrifying time. I'm sure my mother worried all the time about me, especially when the Germans were bombing the Cardiff ports during the Blitz. We all were also terribly worried that Hitler would be invading Britain. Our hospital suffered damage from time to time. We just got used to it. We had so many wounded soldiers to take care of that there was no time to worry.

From time to time, I was able to take a short holiday and make the slow train ride back to Cilgerran see my mother. I arrived home late one afternoon in March of 1944 and found my mother visiting with an old friend of hers in the parlor. We got to talking, and her friend told me about a dance in the YMCA hall [today's Village Hall] that night for the American soldiers who were stationed nearby in Albro Castle—the old workhouse—in St. Dogmaels. (The troops were there preparing for the Normandy invasion that June, but of course we didn't know that at the time.) She urged me to go and have some fun at the dance.

But I refused, saying I had just gotten home and wanted to talk with my mother and then get to bed early after a long day. But she kept insisting: "Oh, but my dear girl, you must go—you never know, you may meet your fate tonight!" My mother agreed, and so they finally persuaded me to go.

And I did meet my fate that night. —*AJS*

Tilla's Story, continued

I stayed up reading a book until Nesta got home from the dance. When she came into the parlor, late it was, but her eyes were sparkling and she wore a big smile. I knew right away that my friend's premonition had come true. Nesta sat down by the fire and told me about this one young man.

He was American, of course, small in stature with red hair and ice blue eyes. Nesta's father had had reddish hair also, so at first I was worried that she was looking for someone to replace him. She went on and on about how nice this soldier was—his name was Bill—and that even though he wasn't the best looking man there that night, there was something about him.... I was always too sensible to believe in "love at first sight," but that night I thought perhaps it could happen.

Bill Johnson, early 1940's

I was of course so happy for her, but you know how mothers can worry about such things. Nesta had a serious boyfriend before, but he would never get around to asking her to marry him, so she had recently broken up with him. It wasn't until the next morning that it hit me that she might marry this man and move to America. My heart almost broke at the thought. But I was determined to let her be, and see where things went. It isn't always easy for a mother to keep quiet, but I knew I had to.

Nesta was home for several days before she had to go back to Cardiff, and she saw Bill a few more times that week. He came to our house so I could meet him, and I must say I liked him very much. He wasn't like a typical American, if you know what I mean. I would have to say we hit it off. He was polite and considerate, and also very wise.

I say "wise" because after Nesta went back to Cardiff, about once a week Bill would borrow a bicycle and ride the six or seven miles from St. Dogmaels to Cilgerran to see me. We got along very well, and by the time Nesta came home again on leave, I knew him better than she did. And I was convinced he was a good man for her. They became engaged before his unit shipped off to France that June. Nesta and I were both so afraid we might never see him again.

Nesta's Story, continued

I was over the moon in love with Bill. It was so hard to leave Cilgerran that time, not knowing when—or even if—I would see him again. He didn't know how long his unit would be in Wales; all he knew is that they would probably be leaving within the year. We promised to write to each other often, and we did. I saw him briefly one or two more times in Cilgerran.

We didn't really talk about it, but I was pretty sure Bill had no plans to stay in Britain after the war was over. I always assumed I would be joining him in America—and in Texas of all places!—at some point.

With a war going on, plans of any kind were impossible to make. Somehow I knew it would all work out. But I couldn't stop worrying about my mother. How could I leave her again?—and this time it would seem like for good. I knew she would never come to America—she had never traveled farther than Cardigan in her entire life! But if I didn't leave, I could not marry Bill. And I knew I couldn't lose him. What a dilemma.

Back at Whitchurch Hospital in Cardiff, the air raids went on for a while and the wounded soldiers kept coming in. They were sad times and good times—good times when the men got better and were released to go back to their home towns. I enjoyed my work and felt I was doing an important job. But all I could think of was Bill.

That June he wrote to tell me his unit was leaving Wales to go to France. Later I learned he was in one of the units participating in the Normandy invasion. When the news of it arrived—and the incredible tragedy of all those good men killed that day—I was terribly anxious. It took a month before I learned that he was not part of the first landing, but instead arrived five days later. But the Allies were still fighting the Germans all over northern France, and Bill was in the middle of it all. It was hard for me to sleep at night.

And then, more than a year later, the war was over. What a joyous day that was for Britain! There was no time to come home to Cilgerran for our wedding, so we made plans to marry in Cardiff, at the little church down the road from my rooming house in Rhiwbina. My dear friend Elizabeth had to practically drag my mother into the train with her. It was August 1945. Bill and I had a few days together before I had to get back to work at the hospital and Bill left for six months of post-war duty in Germany.

Nesta and Bill's wedding, Cardiff, 1945

In March of 1946 I was finally able to get a place on a war brides' ship to America. It left from Southampton, and it was a terribly long and rough journey across the Atlantic. There were several hundred of us young women crowded together along with many, many crying babies and small children. It seems we were all seasick at one time or another.

But Bill was there to meet me when the ship arrived in New York. It seemed like forever since I had seen him. We boarded a train for Chicago to see his aunt and uncle there, and then took another train to Macomb, Illinois, where Bill had grown up. We visited his friends and family, and I really liked the town and the people I met. They were all so nice to me.

I am not sure I was prepared for life in San Antonio, Texas. Bill had told me it was terribly hot there a good part of the year, but I didn't experience that at first, since we had arrived in early April—

though it was still warm enough then! I was a little nervous about meeting his parents, but they were welcoming and very nice to me. We found a small apartment on the second floor of a big old white frame house, and Bill began his job as a clerk at a local Army base.

Oh, it was fine for a while. But once the newness wore off, I became terribly homesick. I often worried, had I made the right decision? Was my mother getting along okay? Bill was a wonderful husband, but life in Texas was so completely different from Wales, and I felt like such a foreigner. And I was alone all day in our hot apartment and had no friends and not much to do except housework. I had enjoyed my work as a nurse, but I learned that my British nursing training was not recognized in the States, so that I would have to start nursing school all over again. And the closest one at that time was several hundred miles away.

Most of all I missed my mother. Bill saw that I needed to go home, and somehow we scraped together enough money. He was able to get time off of work, and we went—this time on the Queen Mary—luxury compared to the troop ship I had come over on! For years after he said that we made that trip to prove to my mother— and to me—that we could come home to see her any time. Of course, that wasn't really true because of the great expense. But it meant so much to me, and to her. (Years later, after Bill retired, we traveled to Cilgerran every summer to be with her. We tried to make up for all the lost time, and I think we did.)

We had a terrible scare on that visit, though. Bill had caught a bad cold on the way over, and it soon got much worse. It aggravated the asthma he had developed during the war, and my mother and I took turns staying up at night with him. One day, Aunty May, my Uncle William Griffiths's second wife, offered to come help take care of him—she had once been a nurse. I think she saved his life, and for that I was forever grateful to her. —*AJS*

Bill and Nesta on the Queen Mary, 1947

Tilla's Story, continued

I thought the world of Bill, so it was not a surprise at all when Nesta told me she wanted to marry him. But it was an agonizing decision for her. Because she knew she would be leaving me behind, she didn't tell him "yes" for several weeks. I told her over and over again that she had to live her own life and that I would be alright. She finally saw that I meant it. "You'll never find another one like that one, my girl," I would tell her. She knew I was right.

She came back a year later for a short visit. It was hard to see her leave again, but I made myself believe that this was just the first of many visits to come. She wanted me to come to Texas, but that was simply out of the question. I have always—except for the time I went to Cardiff for Nesta and Bill's wedding—slept in my own bed.

Around that time, I began seeing an old friend from a neighboring village, David Howell. He had lost his wife years earlier. We married and he moved into Teifi View with me. I know that made Nesta feel better about leaving me again. But, sadly, David died just a few years later.

In early 1961, I had a letter from Nesta with wonderful news. She was coming home for the first time in nearly fourteen years. Bill would have to stay behind, but she would be bringing her two young daughters—Andrea and Marcia—with her to spend the summer here. I practically danced around the village with the good news. I ran up—well, as much as a sixty-three-year-old woman could—to Aberdyfan to tell my mother and my brother, James.

—*AJS*

Nesta and Tilla reunited, 1947

Four generations: Nesta, Andrea, Tilla (standing); Louise and Marcia, 1961

Andrea's Story

That Mysterious Pull

I turned thirteen during that summer in Wales. My sister and I still agree, it was the very best summer of our lives. Uncle James had a car and picked us up at the ferry landing in Fishguard—we had flown from New York to Shannon, and took the train across Ireland to Cork, and then the overnight ferry to Wales.

Our memories of the visit differ, but we both recall how, when we arrived at Teifi View, we were intercepted by a neighbor's daughter outside the house, so that my mother and grandmother could have a private reunion after all those years. The girl was very nice to us, but we could barely understand a word she said. That night before going to bed, I remember telling my mother, "I thought you said people spoke English here." But the girl was speaking English. Within a few days we got used to the accent— and the rest of the village to our strange way of speaking, I am sure.

We loved talking with our grandmother. She was our only grandmother, since our paternal grandmother had died when we were quite young. We loved exploring the woods around the river, playing in the castle, and eating sponge cakes and Grandma's gooseberry pies and Walls ice cream and Cadbury chocolates and wonderful fresh-baked bread, still warm from the bakery. Tea time was our favorite time of day—we never experienced that in Texas! I added a much-needed ten pounds to my scrawny adolescent frame that summer.

It was so beautiful there, even when it rained, which it did a lot. Then we stayed inside by the fire (we were always so cold in that house!) and read Enid Blyton books for hours at a time. I could have stayed there forever. I could not understand how my mother wanted to leave such a wonderful place. Well, there was my dad, of course…. For years after I dreamed of returning to live there, but then real life in the States—college, marriage, a child—intervened.

Twenty years later, I came back, this time with my eleven-year-old daughter. Stephanie and Grandma hit it off right away. They were both so interested in nature. Stephanie had captured some tadpoles during a visit to Ceibwr Bay one day and brought them back to live in Grandma's birdbath. The two of them would keep an eye on the stray cats and tried to protect the tadpoles while they grew into tiny frogs. One day the frogs were gone—hopped away, we hoped.

Then fifty years after our first visit, my sister and I went back one more time together. By then, we were the last of the Mathias women; Louise had died in 1970, Tilla in 1990, and Nesta in 2008. We stayed for a week near Cilgerran and walked around all of our favorite places, soaking in the specialness of that village and our memories of that long-ago summer.

Today, the yearning to spend more time there has returned. The pull seems to be more than family memories and my being half-Welsh. It also has something to do with the area's physical beauty, with its feeling of remoteness, history, and timelessness. It is hard to explain. The Welsh have a word for it: *hiraeth*. --*AJS*

Marcia and Andrea, aboard the Fishguard ferry, 1961

Marcia's Story

I Am Not a Boy!

I was nine years old the summer we went to Wales. I remember Mom telling us that we were finally going to meet Grandma Wales, the person who wrote all those blue letters to Mom. I had never questioned why we called her Grandma Wales—that was just her name. I think I was pretty excited about the trip since I was going to get to fly on an airplane and ride on a big boat for the first time. Pretty big stuff for a little girl!

I recall the plane ride to Shannon, Ireland, on a propeller Pan Am flight. I was in a bad mood because I had to wear a dress on the plane. (However, I was in a bad mood anytime I had to wear a dress.) We had to wait until the evening to catch the overnight ferry from Cork to Wales. As I recall, it was either a Sunday or a holiday because no shops were open. I just remember walking around trying to find someplace open where we could get some food. I'm sure I was driving our mother, Nesta, crazy because I was always hungry and was therefore probably whining and complaining.

Anyway, we finally boarded the ferry and went down to the lowest deck. It was a huge room with bunk beds stacked three high with probably twenty other women and girls there. Each bed had a small box attached to the side. Mom told us it was there in case you got seasick. I'm pretty sure I got the top bunk. Poor Andrea was in the middle bunk and probably wasn't all too happy that night when I did get seasick, but I think everything made it into the box. Most everyone there did get seasick. Looking back, I think I understand why Great-grandma Louise didn't want to take another boat ride. Mom said we got seasick because there was a big swell that night. A swell—now what was that? One of the many new words I would learn that summer in Wales.

When we arrived in Fishguard early the next morning, Uncle James was waiting there to take us to Cilgerran. The first thing I noticed when we got off the boat was the smell. There was a distinct odor in the air, and to this day whenever I smell that odor, I think of Wales. I don't mean that in a bad way, either. It was just the first time I think I had ever smelled diesel fuel. Then as we started driving through Fishguard, I noticed how most of the houses were made of stone and were attached to one another and that they all had chimneys. This was a very strange sight to a girl who was used to seeing only one-level tract houses in Texas. It all looked so grand! Pretty soon another smell was taking over. This time it was the smell of coal from the fireplaces—another odor that to this day I associate with Wales.

When we finally got to Cilgerran, we stopped at Grandma's house, Teifi View, but one of the neighbors said she wasn't inside, that she was down the road working in the vegetable garden. We walked down a ways and saw a woman on the dingle side of the road. Finally, here was Grandma Wales! I remember her hugging us and telling us to watch out for the nettles. (Another new word. A few days later, we found out the hard way what they were.)

We went into Teifi View and I was excited to see that not only did it have a fireplace, but it had an upstairs! The only thing it didn't have was a bathroom. I was a little taken aback by that. But it was fine, the WC outside had a nifty long chain to flush with, not one of those wimpy handles! And we got to take a bath in the kitchen, using a metal tub filled with water heated on the stove. That was definitely fine with me because it meant I didn't have to take a bath every day. The only thing that took getting used to was the chamber pot under the bed. I'm not sure I ever used it, though.

We settled in for a summer of fun. I think the first or second day we were there, Andrea and I explored the village. We absolutely loved the fact that there was a castle that we could play in whenever we wanted. And a river right down a lane from the house! As we were exploring, some boys from the village (who had obviously heard some girls from Texas were coming) asked us if we lived on a ranch and had horses and if there were cowboys and Indians there!

It seemed like the summer days would go on forever. We made friends with a dog, Timmy, and with a black and white cat (was her name Cindy?), who one day delivered a shrew to our front door. Mom said the cat left it there because she liked us.

With our new friend, Timmy, 1961

We would go to the small library in the village and check out Enid Blyton books to read when it was raining or in the evening before bed. (Grandma had only a radio, never a television.) I really believed we would find ourselves in our own kind of mystery adventure there in Cilgerran, so every time we went out to play, my imagination would start looking for an adventure.

For example, Mom and Grandma had told us about a mansion near Llechryd where rich people lived. Well, we wanted to see that, so we walked along the path by the Teifi River until we came to it. I distinctly recall looking through some bushes on to the grounds of the mansion (which I later found out was Castle Malgwyn) and seeing people playing tennis. I made up some story about a small child being held prisoner in that mansion and that somehow Andrea and I would save him or her.

When we were playing at the castle, I imagined that we would find a dungeon with someone trapped in it or maybe a secret passageway that led to someplace exciting.

On the Teifi River

We would play down by the river, too, and I desperately wanted to go swimming in it (when you're a kid, any body of water is inviting, no matter how cold) but we were told we could never go swimming there because of the eddies. Yet another new word to add to my vocabulary. Mom told us that some children had drowned in the river, and she alluded to the fact that that would be our fate if we ever swam there.

I recall walking to Great-grandma's house, Aberdyfan, a few times. I remember Mom telling me when I was older that I had worn pants on one of my visits and Great-grandma had made the disparaging remark to Mom, "I thought you had two girls." So I had to wear a dress on all our other visits to see her. I recall having our picture taken together. Mom said it was rare that a family had a four-generation photograph. Of course, she had to explain to me what that meant.

That summer, like most good things, ended all too soon. The journey back home was a little less eventful, and we were soon once again enduring the Texas heat. Although I did return to Wales in 1970 and 1975, neither trip would match the magic of the first one. However, the trip with my sister in 2011 did come fairly close, and I look forward to a time when I can return again. —*MLM*

Marcia and Andrea in front of Teifi View, Cilgerran, 2011

Elizabeth on the Teifi banks; she wrote on the back, "Remember this place?"

Elizabeth's Story

At Last, a Happy Ending

I was a life-long friend of Nesta's. We knew each other for almost eighty years. Like her, I was also was born in Cilgerran in 1921. My parents were older than most, for they had been hoping for a long time to have a child. I was their first and only.

Oh, how they doted on me! People said I was a very pretty little girl. When I was about seven years old, my father read in the newspaper that a children's beauty contest was being held in Cardigan. He was sure I would win! But I needed a fancy dress, and we had no money to buy one or even sew one. My father was a milk delivery man. Part of his job was to collect money from his customers. He decided that he would "borrow" just enough from the till to buy a dress for me. He wasn't a dishonest man, for he fully meant to pay it all back, just little by little.

To tell the truth, I have no memory of the contest at all. But I do know the results—my father was caught. The dairy company accused him embezzling money. He was fired immediately. I was too little to really understand what happened, but I recall the other children taunting me in school after that. The entire village knew our family's shame. If we were poor before that, we were destitute after. A few of the villagers helped us out as much as they could—but most people were poor in those days. My father found jobs here and there over the years, but he never had a good job after that one. No one ever forgot his mistake.

When I was seventeen, I was able to get a scholarship to go to nursing school. Then World War II broke out. I was working in a hospital in North Wales at the time. I met a soldier and fell in love. We were married shortly after the war. But sadly, just before our wedding, I got to know his best friend—our best man—and fell deeply in love with him. But what could I do? I had to go through with the wedding. I already had caused enough shame on my family.

I was surely punished for my wicked thoughts, for two years later both I and my husband contracted tuberculosis. He quickly died of it, while I recovered. But I had to quit the nursing profession, for I could still spread the disease to my patients. I returned home to live with my parents in Cilgerran. By then my mother was very ill and soon died. We were living in a council house, on the dole as they say. Then my dear father lost his eyesight, and I took care of him for many years, until he died in the 1980's. I was all alone, an old woman with no family at all.

Then around 1990, a most wonderful thing happened. One day I received a letter from the man I had loved so truly nearly a half a century earlier. His wife had recently died, and he was wondering how I was doing. He came to see me and soon after we were married. I had to wait until I was in my seventies to find real happiness.

Some people may think that I led a very sad life—but then some people never find joy in their entire life. I was so happy and grateful for what I finally had. —*AJS*

Home

Lyndhurst

Lyndhurst. What a grand-sounding name for a Victorian-style middle-class home in Cilgerran. But it deserved to have a grand name. Lyndhurst was indeed a prize—a final reward for generations of backbreaking work carried out by Griffiths men at Cilgerran's Dolbadau Quarry.

On the outside Lyndhurst was grey, the color of a winter sky. If it hadn't been attached to other terraced houses one might have missed it altogether. "But once through the door," my mother used to say, "the house was ablaze with color," painted with the stories and laughter of my great-grandfather, William Griffiths, whom his grandchildren and great-grandchildren knew simply as "Data"—their family word for grandfather.

Data's family didn't always live at Lyndhurst. After his wife, Hannah, died, Data set to work to make new and happier memories for his four children and himself. He bought a pub called The Castle on High Street in Cilgerran, a few houses away from their old house, Clifton. He remodeled The Castle into a modern and comfortable home with an upstairs toilet—unheard of!

His daughter Pat insisted that their new home have a change of name; she didn't want her house to sound like the pub it used to be. Data agreed and christened their new home Lyndhurst, after a beautiful house Pat had read about in a favorite book.

Lyndhurst's roof was made of slate shingles from Dolbadau Quarry. They were all hand cut by the Griffiths men and Data himself. He laid riven slate on the floors of rooms downstairs and hand polished the smooth slate fireplace mantle. His personal touch was everywhere, and that made Data's house very much their family home.

In the back garden of Lyndhurst, Data ran an egg business. He kept his hens in cages made of wooden dowels and stacked them on top of each other. He also built a small shop on one side of the house so that his son, Titus, could run a fish and chips business from home when his asthma kept him from the quarry. Lyndhurst was where two of Data's children welcomed their own children into the world. Sarah Mary's sons, Willie and Kai Larsen, and Titus's daughters, Shirley and Enid Griffiths, were all born in an upstairs bedroom at Lyndhurst.

The heart of the house was its fireplace. Often a simple supper would turn into a lively evening of song and storytelling with Data sharing a funny tale of something that happened at the quarry or in the village. He was a master storyteller, and he delighted his friends and family with his tall tales and animated movements.

In our family if one possessed the gift of master storytelling it was said that he or she had "a gift of the *hwyl*." The gift of the *hwyl* had been passed down in our DNA for generations. Data had it; Sarah Mary and Titus had it; Willie and Nora Larsen had it. Sadly, I think the gift of the *hwyl* died in our branch of the family when my mother, Nora, passed away.

Above the mantel at Lyndhurst was a large oval photograph of Data's wife, Hannah Thomas Griffiths. The photograph was the work of a relative by marriage, Cilgerran photographer Tom Mathias. The treasured photograph of my great-grandmother, which I longed to see but never did, was discarded by Data's second wife, May.

Close to the fireplace, in a *cwtch* under the stairs, was an ancient Welsh oak settle, which had been in the Griffiths family since the beginning of time. Mamgu—our name for Data's mother, who was my great-great-grandmother, Martha Evans Griffiths—sat on that settle for years, with her black and white apron across her lap, traditional plaid shawl over her shoulders, hands folded gently and her lips set in a perpetual smile.

Mamgu's withered face, my mother said, reflected the dancing light from the fire. She recalled that as a little girl she would sit for hours on a small stool in front of Mamgu and stare, transfixed, at her great-grandmother's wizened, glowing features and gentle smile.

Mamgu's settle seat lead a double life—the lid opened up to store toys for the Griffiths children. Regrettably, although Data's will stated that the remains of his estate were to be given to his children after May's death, Mamgu's settle, along with the house and all the family's furniture, was sold at auction to pay for May's last days in a nursing home. No notice was given to anyone in the Griffiths family.

I never saw Lyndhurst for myself when it was part of the Griffiths estate, but I knew every *cwtch* and cranny of Data's Cilgerran home from the stories told by my mother and grandmother.

For many years I was sad that I was never able to see my great-grandmother's picture or sit by Data's fireplace. But after learning about that auction, I decided that it was best, after all, that I knew Lyndhurst only through my family's memories.

It is said that if you want to remember what a deceased loved one looked like in the prime of her health, you should never view her in her coffin. To me, Lyndhurst will forever be remembered as "grey on the outside, ablaze with the color of laughter on the inside." I never "viewed" her any other way. —*KGM*

Martha Evans Griffiths ("Mamgu") her son William Griffiths ("Data"), 1930
(both Tom Mathias)

Family

Griffiths

William's Story

For Love

Author's Note: I must confess I never met my great-grandfather William Griffiths; I was a small child when he died in 1954. I know him only through the recollections of my mother, aunts, and cousins. The story that follows is how it was told to me, and I repeat it here as accurately as I can. I sincerely hope that it will offend no one, and that readers will come to know a little about a very human man who was born more than 134 years ago.

Unlike so many people who lived in Welsh villages around the turn of the last century, my great-grandfather, William Griffiths, appeared to have married for love, not convenience—twice. He said he considered himself a lucky man.

In 1900, when William was twenty-one, he married Hannah Thomas of Llechryd, despite his parents' reservations. Together the young couple prospered and created a family of four children. Sadly, Hannah could not join him in watching them grow into adults, for she died before her fortieth birthday.

After Hannah's death in 1917, William devoted himself to caring for his children and working to keep the family business, Dolbadau Quarry, going at a time when slate quarries in West Wales were closing down. Remarriage was not on his mind. His two younger daughters were just ten and eleven years old, and his son was fifteen—he did not want to subject them to the potential horrors of a stepmother. His eldest daughter, Sarah Mary, was sixteen and took over running the household in her mother's place.

Within a decade, all of William's children were grown. His insistence that they become well-educated had paid off. They all were safely embedded in middle-class Britain and would be able to pursue lives that he and Hannah only dreamed of as children of the working class. Louisa and Pat had earned honors degrees, and Pat even went on to win her master's degree. Titus was an able businessman and was handling the quarry accounts. Sarah Mary, who had chosen marriage over university, was as capable and independent as any woman he had ever known. William was, indeed, a lucky man. He had done a good job.

He was lucky, he knew, that he had been able to rear his family before his quarry stopped producing slate. He had put aside some savings—enough to privately educate all his grandchildren—for what he hoped would be the second generation of well-educated Griffithses. Education was "the thing" in William's mind, and he assured his children that private educations would be his gift to his beloved grandchildren.

When William's son, Titus, married Edith Jones in 1929, the couple agreed to live with William at Lyndhurst. It would take the efforts of the father and the son working alongside each other to keep Dolbadau Quarry afloat for as long as they could. But the late 1930's brought big changes to the lives of the Griffiths family.

By 1938, as predicted, the quarry had produced her last load. All the equipment was sold and the offices packed up. Titus found work right away; he was a young and clever man. But William felt his life was finished. He was lost. He was no longer an involved father or an important employer.

A year later, the Griffiths family went through even more great changes. Two wars broke out: WWII and the Griffiths family private war. The second one started when Edith's unmarried sister, May, a forty-one year-old nurse, moved back to Cilgerran. She naturally visited Edith often at Lyndhurst. And that was the start of the problem.

William seemed to enjoy May's visits more than anyone. He found himself feeling important again. But as his fondness for May grew, William's children became less fond of her...very much less fond of her, in fact. To make matters worse, Titus and Edith began to feel torn by loyalties, him to his father and her to her sister.

Tensions grew. Seeing where the relationship between his father and his sister-in-law was heading, Titus moved his family out of Lyndhurst and into a bungalow called High Fields, which he had built about a mile up the road in Pen-y-Bryn. He and his family became "outsiders" at Lyndhurst. Sarah Mary, Pat and Louise, though living elsewhere, also found themselves on the perimeter of their father's world, while May found a permanent place within it. The entire family, William included, was distraught about the rift but could find no way forward.

May, William, and friends, c.1950

One day a nosy neighbor settled everything—or so the recollection of one family member goes. When she got no answer at William's door, she entered the house and found William and May in a compromising position. In an instant, William and May became the talk of the town. William was a dutiful man of solid Victorian values, even if he broke them occasionally, and he could not allow his actions to stain May's reputation or the Griffiths name. So the couple traveled to Narberth, where they were quietly married in the registry office.

William believed that a dutiful husband must provide for his wife until the end of her days. Because of their twenty-year age difference, he knew that May would outlive him by a long time, so he did the right thing by her once again. He changed his will. All that he had so carefully saved to provide a legacy for his children and grandchildren was suddenly redirected to ensure a life-long income for May. It is safe to say his children were not pleased. The family was fractured.

The four Griffiths children remained close, visiting each other often and corresponding by letter. They all were on speaking terms with their father, but, sadly, the once-close relationship they had would never recover from the "intrusion" of May. Although years later it seemed that none of them carried resentment over losing their inheritance, they always felt cheated out of their relationship with their father.

William kept up with his grandchildren as much as circumstances would allow. To their credit, his children wanted their children to benefit from being a part of his world, even if they were not. He passed on his mantra, if not his money, to them: "Edooocation, Mun, Edooocation, see!

May lived to be ninety-nine years old, outliving three of William's four children. She lived alone in Lyndhurst for more than forty years after William's death in 1954. She secluded herself in the house knowing that the villagers did not look kindly on her for depriving her stepchildren of their family inheritance.

And William's grandchildren? Each one of them—all six— went on to university to become teachers. They made William, by his own standards, a lucky man indeed! —*KGM*

Nesta Griffiths and her cousin, Enid Griffiths, daughter of Titus and Edith Griffiths and granddaughter of William Griffiths, 1931 (Tom Mathias)

Pat Griffiths and Nesta Griffiths, c. 1940

Martha Hannah's (Pat's) Story

Lessons Learned

L ife in our Pembrokeshire village was luckier for me than for many other village children of the early 1900's. My father, William Griffiths, owner of the Dolbadau Slate Quarry in Cilgerran, saw the coming demise of working class jobs in rural West Wales and prepared his children for change. As the slate in the quarries dwindled, my father knew that the industry was on its last legs and that the hard working masons and slaters of Pembrokeshire would soon be struggling for work. He encouraged us to rise above our stations in life so that we could enjoy the freedom and prosperity that advancing to the middle class would offer.

In those days, just about the only way a working-class child could move up was by becoming a preacher, a teacher or a nurse. So William Griffiths's children were given a steady diet of books, which we read from dawn to dusk all day, every day, to prepare us. My sister Louisa and I loved to learn—our father made it seem like fun. But he also made it mandatory. In the end, my father's plan for our futures succeeded. Louisa and I received several degrees in education from University College of Wales, in Aberystwyth. Those degrees were, indeed, our passports to freedom.

Although village life had little to offer me academically, the strong family values and village wisdom of Cilgerran gave me everything else I needed to become a capable woman. Welsh culture and traditional values had molded my character. The addition of education opened my mind. The combination became the backbone of my life.

Having a husband and children of my own was of no interest to me. Learning was my love. Teaching was my passion. As a headmistress at some of the best schools for girls, I devoted my life to hundreds of "daughters" who went on to build successful lives and contribute much to the world.

Perhaps ahead of my time, I pushed for equal rights and higher education for all women. Included in the education of "my girls" was the teaching of traditional women's crafts and homemaking skills. Those were, I taught them, priceless treasures. Acquiring and preserving women's traditional skills were equally as important as the attainment of rights and formal education for the advancement of women.

Almost all of my father's children, grandchildren, great-grandchildren, and great-great-grand-children have become educators. Father's words have been genetically coded in Griffiths DNA and I couldn't be more proud: "Edoocation, Mun! See? Edoocation!"

At the end of my career, I came home to Wales and joined my sister Louisa in living out our last years. Both of us had traveled the world, taught hundreds of girls and shared the experience of growing up in a traditional family in a small rural village in Pembrokeshire. My life still held importance to my sister, and I was glad to come home. After all my years of teaching, you see, I had learned the most important lesson of my own life, and I will share it with you now:

"The people of West Wales sing in our blood. Listen, and enjoy their voices." —*KGM*

Pat at the beach, 1920's; Pat, Sarah Mary, and Nora, c. 1970

Sarah Mary Griffiths, two weeks old, Cilgerran, 1900

Sarah Mary's Story

The Ties That Bind

The great thing about being a granddaughter is that you get to know your grandmother in ways that your mother never knew her—at least I did. Although she was a mother of three and grandmother of six, my grandmother, Sarah Mary Griffiths Larsen, was "just mine" in many ways. We were separated by the Atlantic Ocean for much of my life, but I always felt we were never far apart. She was one of the people who loved me, even when she was angry with me. I adored her.

Through my mother's eyes and those of my Uncles Kai and Willie, Sarah Mary was a strict disciplinarian. She was an iron-willed woman who brought up her family by enforcing the Victorian values she grew up with in West Wales. Her mission: to rear well-brought-up, successful children with university educations. Sarah Mary expected each member of her family to do his or her duty. There was much time for work, little time for play. And when they did play, they played by her rules.

But I never knew *that* Sarah Mary. In my eyes, Grandma was a free-spirited best friend with boundless energy and twinkling eyes. She had a great sense of play and her quick wit kept us in stitches all day. Besides sharing the joy of laughter, we discussed everything and anything. She shared family secrets with me—things my mother never knew—because, she said, I was special.

Grandma was a master storyteller. She had a real gift of the *hwyl*. Her stories were usually hilarious and embellished by animated expressions. But I always wanted to know the true stories about her life, not just the entertaining ones that people loved to hear.

I would ask her things like, "What was it like to grow up in the old days, what was it like to be a little girl in Cilgerran, what was it like to go to school there, what did it feel like to have a dead mother?"

I asked question upon question, and each answer peeled away another layer of the mystery that was Sarah Mary. I was determined to find Grandma, but the road to finding the real, true Sarah Mary was full of unexpected surprises.

Sarah Mary started her life with a secret she wanted no one to know. Her parents, William Griffiths and Hannah Thomas, didn't marry until she was a year old. The fact that she was born "on the wrong side of the blanket" was not that unusual in 1900's Wales, but she was humiliated by it.

When Sarah Mary's mother died at the age of forty, one of the first things Sarah Mary did was burn the family's silver-cornered bible. It contained a written record of births and deaths of generations of Griffithses, including her own. If she got rid of the thing, she thought, she could burn her away her secret. But in Cilgerran secrets could never be burned away, and in Sarah Mary's mind she was "marked."

Sarah Mary inherited the love of laughter from both her mother and her father, but in her small village of Cilgerran she would often have to invent her own comedy. She said to me, when I was a teenager, "You and your sister Christi, your cousins Andrea and Marcia —you all think that our lives in Cilgerran were enchanted and magical. But your visions of Welsh life in a small village are made of fantasies. My real-life memories are quite different! We had some good days, but to me, trying to survive in a small village was often akin to hell."

She went on, "Now, I'll tell you how I survived in my small village. I studied people, see, and learned to mimic just about everyone in Cilgerran and Llechryd. I listened for the music in their conversations, watched their expressions on their faces and mimicked their quirks and idiosyncrasies—until I 'became them.' My friends and family dissolved into fits of laughter when I pretended to be the people they knew. Like my father, I could tell a good story. Like so many of the Welsh, I could create a mackerel from a minnow—in an instant."

Grandma didn't like to think that mimicking the villagers was unkind. When she learned that I had passed down to my nieces and nephew the stories she told of Cilgerran folk, she gave herself credit for making them immortal. And she was right. Five generations and almost a hundred years later, Sarah Mary's great-great-grandchildren in Texas know how Ethel Annie Griffiths looked when she sang at the Eisteddfod in 1918.

I have mimicked Grandma's story of Ethel Annie more times than I can count, complete with heaving bosom, popping eyes and a whale-sized mouth that could easily have held a dozen eggs when she opened it to sing. Thanks to Grandma, villagers like Ethel Annie have been given everlasting life.

Pubs were off limits in Grandma's world. She hated even the thought of alcohol and she voiced her disapproval in no uncertain terms. I never realized how she strongly she had passed on her disdain of pubs until my mother, Nora, and I traveled back to Cilgerran when Mom was in her sixties.

I suggested that we have a snack at the Pendre Inn, down the street from Lyndhurst, where my mother spent her childhood summers. But Mom could hardly cross the Pendre's threshold; she could tangibly feel her mother's disapproval. She was visibly shaken as she entered the forbidden pub that was, all those years ago, a tabooed area of her childhood landscape.

Sarah Mary, it turned out, had good reason for keeping her children away from pubs and alcohol. She wanted to protect them from a disease that she recognized might have run in her family. Sarah Mary had another secret.

"All of us kept secrets from each other in the village. We had to. Gossip was highly sought after entertainment, and none of us wanted to be the star of the show. I helped my mother keep a secret, see—a big one! *Duw, Duw,* how shall I say this? My mother had a weakness…she was fond of the bottle!"

She went on to tell me a story I had never heard before. This time it was not a funny story. There was no laughter, no animation. She was trying to pick her words carefully so as not to paint her beloved mother, Hannah, in a bad light. It was time, though, she thought, to warn me of dangers that might trap me if I was not vigilant about abstaining from alcohol.

"When I was a little girl," Grandma recalled, "my mother would send me down the road to a pub called The Black to fetch a small bottle, which I was told to hide under my overcoat. I was warned that if I told my father or anyone else of our secret, she would put me in the attic with the bats. I was terrified. So I made the trips to the pub many times, checking to be sure no one saw me, just as instructed. On the way I always tried to find something funny to lift my spirits and help me forget my fears of getting caught.

One day my father found out that I had been going to The Black for my mother. He wanted it to stop, for my sake as well as hers and the rest of the family's too. He told me I was not allowed to make another trip to the pub—ever! I told him I had to go or Mum would put me in the attic with the bats. My mild and gentle father, who usually had only the kindest words to say to anyone, shocked me when he told me that if I went to The Black again for my mother, he'd put me in the attic with the bats himself!

As our Girl Guides leader often said to us when any living creature was found in a trap, "CRU-EL-TY-TO-AN-I-MALS-AND-THAT-WE-CAN-NOT-HAVE!" I thought of her...I was trapped.

My mother, who came from the neighboring village of Llechryd, probably felt trapped too. Perhaps that's why she married my father—to escape village life in Llechryd. Perhaps that's why she drank when she lived in Cilgerran—to escape having to rear four children in a small Welsh village. The truth was, lots of people secretly drank in Cilgerran. The trick was not to have anyone in your own family be one of them!"

Sarah Mary's father had a plan that would cure her mother of her tendency toward the tipple, enable his family to keep up appearances and offer them salvation. He insisted that the Griffiths family spend every Sunday at Babell Church where they could be seen to be upstanding citizens and hear the fire and brimstone sermons that were sure to keep them from sinning—until the next time.

But the plan backfired as far as Sarah Mary was concerned. She was tired of feeling trapped, and the hell-fire sermons made her feel worse. So she imposed her own ban on church services and pubs.

"One Sunday, when I was thirteen, the vicar put on his most pious face and thundered out, "Sarah Mary Griffiths, come forward to the altar and confess your sins publicly!"

I was mortified—I hadn't sinned at all—but then all those proper people thought I had! The preacher lied. I looked around at all the faces that expected me to say I had done something wicked, then whispered sheepishly, 'No I won't!'

Sunday school class, Babell Chapel, Cilgerran (Tom Mathias)

He persisted by pounding his fist on the pulpit and bellowing, "Sarah Mary Griffiths! Do you want to save your soul from hell? Come forward and be saved!"

I was angry then, see, and yelled back, "No! I do NOT want to be saved!"

I ran out of church that day in tears, and no one could make me go back ever again. What for! Lying was a sin and I didn't need a liar to tell me what was right or wrong. He wasn't a proper parson, you know, to trap people like that!"

Grandma was a complex woman. As strict as most of her values were and as intolerant as she was of alcohol, she could be surprisingly open-minded and very liberal when one least expected it.

One summer when I was visiting her as a teenager, the whole of Great Britain was suffering a hot spell. I wished I had brought my swimming gear and said so to my grandmother.

"*Diawl*, who needs a swimming costume at your age, girl? Just go down to the water and swim in your knickers."

Huh?

"You've nothing to hide at your age, no sags or bags or lumps or bumps—a young girl's body is a beautiful thing and you'll only have it once. Soon it will be too late to swim freely—you'll have to cover it all up!" Hmmm…Grandma really did hate feeling trapped, even by a bathing costume!

Later, on another visit when I had just turned twenty-four, Grandma revealed that she was a little worried that I might not marry. I was, she had confided in my mother, "losing the bloom of youth."

What she was really worried about, though, was not my advancing age as a single woman. She was worried that at my age I may not have remained "untouched." Perhaps no man would have me!

Knowing that Grandma was intent on gauging the level of my purity, I decided not to be not at all forthcoming about my private life. Instead, I planned to amuse myself with her struggle to extract that information. Her attempts actually created a reversal of who got informed of what. Instead of Grandma learning about me, I found out more about the private lives of rural women of the early twentieth century than I ever cared to know.

"Village folk were only human you know," she explained. "There wasn't much to do in the evenings but to go up to Cilgerran Castle, or down to the Teifi or, for some, the pubs. And there were consequences if one waited too long to marry, see. If you played…you paid. There was little a woman could do to prevent getting in the family way.

Your grandfather Kai and I had planned a life of travel and adventure when we first got married. We had moved into my father's home to save our money and build our dreams. We had them too, see, the same as you.

Our plans did not include children in the beginning. But the sheep's gut 'protection gear' we had then wasn't effective, and with so many family members living under one roof people had to jump on an opportunity for private time, whenever or wherever it presented itself. Often people were 'unprepared.' Families just happened. And then they grew and grew and people became more and more trapped by their lives. Sometimes women felt desperate and tried to free themselves."

As my grandmother told her next story, she became pensive and her face grew somber. When she spoke, I understood, perhaps for the first time, some of the burdens and hardships women had endured for generations…and I became very grateful that I had been born in a more modern, forgiving world.

"Oh, how I missed my mother when she left us. Father said she died of 'milk leg,' which in your modern language would be known as "pulmonary embolism."

But village tongues wagged. A hurtful rumor spread throughout the village and eventually reached Sarah Mary. Her mother, they said, died trying to spare their family from an unwanted pregnancy.

"We'll never know if that rumor was true or not; I doubt that it was. But I wouldn't want you to think unkindly of any of the women who had to choose termination. They were often desperate and that was the only solution, then, for themselves and the people they loved. In every village there were women who helped other women 'in that way.' One never, ever, spoke of these things— except secretly, of course!" She went on, "I often wondered how many hydrangea plants were actually sad tributes covering up little secrets."

Grandma's mother was often ill. Sometimes, Hannah wasn't up to tending her four young children. Sarah Mary, being the oldest, was expected to take her young siblings to school with her, watch over them and keep them quiet while she tried to concentrate on her schoolwork. If one of them cried or became noisy during class, the teacher would punish Sarah Mary by standing her in the soot-filled empty fireplace.

Girls wore sparkling white pinafores over their dresses in those days, so when Sarah Mary got home from school she was in big trouble! Her mother had to wash the soot from her pinafore on a scrubbing board.

Cilgerran school, early 1900's (Tom Mathias)

After her mother died, Sarah Mary knew it was her duty to help her father rear her two sisters, Louisa and Pat, and her brother Titus. But she didn't want to be trapped in a small village with children—she wanted to travel the world. Soon, she thought she had discovered a way.

Several young Danish men had come to cut timber at Coedmor, near Cilgerran. The story was that these lads chopped wood for the WWI cause instead of bearing arms against other men. My grandfather, Kai Larsen, was one of them.

"Lots of suitors had come my way," Grandma said, "but to me they were only half-a-man each. I wasn't interested in any of them until I met my dashing Danish tree-feller, Kai Larsen." Kai was blond, blue-eyed, an art student and, best of all, he was foreign. He knew nothing of Cilgerran culture. Marrying a foreigner, she imagined, would be almost like traveling to another country—as Kai's wife, she could liberate herself from her fate in Cilgerran.

"Kai and I married in Cardigan when I was eighteen. Back then British law required that a woman who married a foreigner must become a citizen of the same country as her husband. How exotic, I thought. I looked forward to being Danish. And then we returned from the registry office to live with my father William and brother and sisters...still in Cilgerran! *Duw, Duw!* I was Danish but I wasn't!

I wanted to start my new adventure as a married woman in a faraway place. But soon I became pregnant with Willie and his twin brother. I was trapped again, and this time so was Kai. The pregnancy was difficult. Labor came early and I lost one of the twins. Father removed my still baby from our bedroom, and Kai laid little blue Willie in the open bottom dresser drawer near me.

Kai and Sarah Mary Larsen, on their wedding day, 1919

Father tried to prepare Kai for my death. The custom, I heard him explain to Kai, was that if Willie lived and I died, my infant son would be set on top of my coffin at my burial service. He would be christened at my funeral so that his mother's body could be with him at the most important event of his life. If I died and Willie died too, he and his twin would be laid in my arms for burial in the same coffin. Poor Kai, he couldn't hold back his tears, not even for my sake.

Willie, one year old; Willie and Kai, 1925

Our neighbors laid hay on the street outside the house so that the sounds of the horse carts would not disturb me. As they passed our home, the villagers fell silent and the men tipped their hats toward the upstairs window where Willie and I were sleeping. They were respectful of what happened all too often to young people in rural Wales: early death.

But we lived! Willie and I surprised them all. Eventually I gave birth to another son, named Kai after his father. We were still living with my father at our family home.

Finally good luck came our way. Kai found work as a commercial artist in Glamorgan painting advertisements on buildings. We moved our little family to our very own flat in South Wales, and I was free of Cilgerran life at last!

In 1925, soon after I became pregnant with our daughter Nora, Kai received word that he must return to Denmark for a family emergency. He left for Copenhagen and planned to stay for one month. But when his boat docked and the Danish Immigration Authority came on board to check passports, he was arrested for not completing compulsory enlistment time in the Danish army."

My mother, Nora, was born in Gorseinon while her father was held under temporary arrest in Denmark. Sarah Mary had no friends or relatives in her new flat, so when she started labor early she found herself delivering her daughter alone.

"I was playing the piano, see, just as my mother had taught me. The room was chilly for the boys so I stood up to get some coal for the fire. Your mother just went 'knock, knock, knock' at the door…and there she was! I bent over, gave her a hand out into the world, cleaned her up, fed her, wrapped her in my Welsh nursing awl, gave the boys their tea and then went back to play my piano. No bother at all.

My children and I struggled without Kai's income. We learned to be thrifty to the point of being misers and made do with practically nothing. Going without taught me to pinch pennies the rest of my life. I always reminded myself of my mother's words: 'Take care of the pennies and the pounds will take care of themselves!'

My father had always promised to pay for educating my children, but then those promises of support were withdrawn, to afford financial security for my new stepmother—a young woman about my own age. You know the story; it's been repeated for centuries.

I never forgot the constant urging of my father, though: "Edooocation, Mun! Edooocation, see?" I didn't have a university education, but I applied his philosophy when planning for our children's futures. Kai and I vowed to enroll them in grammar school even without my father's contribution. We would push them to university degrees so that they would never be trapped in their lives. To fund that ambition, my husband found work near Whitney in Oxfordshire when he returned from Denmark, and we moved to England. England!

Kai and Willie, Cilgerran, 1930 (Tom Mathias)

Again I found myself in a small rural village, but this time there was a difference: WWII was on Britain's doorstep. Something else was different, too. I had landed an important job with the British Government and I would be contributing to the family income.

The British Council, which had moved its records from central London to rural Oxfordshire for safe-keeping, hired me, Sarah Mary from Cilgerran, to work in their public relations department. It was an odd placement for a shy and insecure young mother of three, but I was back on top of my game! I was a big fish in a small pond and proud of my independence.

But we were very poor, still, during WWII. Kai shared his job with two other men. His work was divided into three jobs so that three families could put food on their tables. Lots of jobs were divided up during the war; it was the right thing to do.

Kai cycled miles to and from work every day and we managed…barely. I put to use what I had learned in Cilgerran: I raised a garden, preserved eggs, slaughtered chickens, all while working a fulltime job and rearing three children.

My childhood in a small Welsh village had taught me so much of what I *didn't* want in life that it was, indeed, my salvation. Our move to London after the war offered me everything I had ever wanted. We were lucky. When the British Council returned their records to London, they moved Kai and me to London with them. We had truly escaped rural life—it was our time to catch up on living!

Sarah Mary and Kai at Buckingham Palace

In London we made friends with interesting people, famous people even, and found ourselves busy attending society events and dancing at more balls than I ever dreamed existed. Since we both loved Old Tyme Dancing, we danced a lot and even gave dance instructions on BBC TV once or twice.

Once we were even invited to Buckingham Palace, where Kai danced with Queen Elizabeth II. She wore a gorgeous ball gown made of tiny gold sequin leaves. Your granddad popped one loose from Her Majesty's dress to give to you as he swirled her around the ballroom...at least that was what he told you. Really, though, he found it on the floor. He framed it himself and gave it to you for your eleventh birthday. You were thrilled.

I would say, all in all, that my life, which started out accidentally in a small Pembrokeshire village in Wales, turned out to be a purposeful one—a good one! And our dreams of travel came true, too.

Now, girl. Don't forget where you put my lucky rabbit's foot! Keep it close while you write this story. Maybe you'll be lucky and someone will read it." —*KGM*

Sarah Mary, 1985

Sarah Mary's Story, continued

Quantum Grandma: Sarah Mary in a Nutshell

"D*uw duw, fach!* You've been at the kitchen table working on your homework since I left for the shops."

"I can't figure out this Bell's Theorem paper, Grandma. I HATE this stupid theorem stuff! Maybe Dad can help me when he gets home."

"Well now, if I were you, I'd just write down, "pi r square" and be done with it, see! Ol' physics! Write down 'pi r square' and your teacher will know you're not as *twp* as you look."

"Quit joking around, Grandma. This is serious. Bell's Theorem, it says here...an invisible stream of energy that will always connect any two objects that have been connected in any way in the past. It says—"

"Well now, I can tell you exactly what that means, my girl. I'm not daft, you know! That Bell's Theorem thing is like when your mother was going into labor with you here in Texas. I was thousands of miles away, visiting in Llechryd with Aunty Pat, when I started having labor pains, too, see—at exactly the same time. And they continued until your mother was out of labor. Pat had to rush me to the doctor.

It may be called 'Bell's Thingy' now, but in my day it was called "sympathy pains." It means we are all connected no matter how far apart we are. Think of an invisible cord running through you to your mother, from your mother through me."

"But, Grandma, that's not..."

"Yes, my girl, we are invisibly connected! Wherever you go, whatever you do, I'll be watching you!

Now! Stay out of trouble!" —*KGM*

Annie Louisa's (Lou's) Story

Please Give Me a Sign

Aunty Lou, this is my fourth straight day on the witness stand in a Welsh court of law. I believe I am doing right by you, but I need some reassurance that I am doing what you want. Send me a sign: slam a door, stop the rain or make the thunder clap three times. Please, do anything at all to tell me that you approve of what I am doing.

It is hard to send a man to prison—especially the handsome lawyer who you once said was "like a son" to you. Is sending him to jail for embezzling your fortune what you want me to do? Or would punishing this dishonorable man break your heart even more?

You have made me executor of your will, so I must be sure your final wishes are carried out. But clouds of doubt are closing in on me as the end of the trial draws near. If we win this case, the man you cared for and trusted will spend many years behind bars. I am not sorry for him, but I am terribly sorry that he hurt you.

You worked so hard all your life to realize to your dreams. And although you lived to be ninety-one, many of those dreams died when you were a young woman. A lesser person would have given up, but you've fought your battles bravely and without complaint. Now you have left us and it is my honor to fight your last battle for you.

You were so young when your mother died. Data, I know, did his best to be a mother and a father to his children. He encouraged you to attend university in Aberystwyth. You and Aunty Pat were the first of our Griffiths family to earn degrees. When you left Cilgerran and married Jim Hughes, you must have thought the life you had always dreamed of had just begun. Within a short time Uncle Jim was vice president of a bank in Bangor and you landed a post as a English teacher at the Bangor Girls School.

In your beautiful home with your handsome husband your biggest dream of all finally came true—you gave birth to a little girl. She was a beauty, complete with huge blue eyes, strawberry blond ringlets and a sharp mind. She was perfect! Margaret was a "Daddy's girl" and you were in love with both of them.

Who would have thought that when Margaret was a young teenager, her father would die? History had repeated itself. Just like you, Margaret ended up with one parent, and like just like your father you took on the role of two parents. You must have felt your daughter's pain so deeply having been through the same trauma yourself.

Your tiny body, barely five feet tall, held the heart of a lion. Although Uncle Jim left you financially secure, you continued your career of teaching school and educated yourself about finance and investing. You put money aside for Margaret's education and her financial security, just in case something happened to you. All your hopes and dreams became tied to Margaret's happiness and her success.

When Margaret was an older teenager she began to change. Not in the normal way that teenagers become rebellious, but in a way that her mood swings became "out of control." There were rumors about her mental health, and you became very protective of her and her privacy. Sometimes you suffered broken arms, had bad falls and black eyes. No one dared to wonder if Margaret might have had anything to do with those accidents. Having someone think ill of Margaret would have hurt you much more deeply than any of your injuries ever could.

It felt like a knife in your heart, you said, when Margaret was diagnosed with cervical cancer. Forty-three years of age was too young for any woman to die, especially one so cherished. You kept your head held high through your grief, not wanting pity or sympathy from any of us, but we could see your heart was broken and we were helpless.

Somehow you managed to keep your wicked sense of humor and your positive outlook on life. You were, indeed, one of the strongest women I have ever known. Courage ran in the Griffiths women. Each and every one of you was a kind and lovely lady on the outside but a fierce warrior within.

In your seventies, when you lost your eyesight completely and became very frail, we were all worried for your safety. A load was taken off our minds when your sister, Pat, moved from Llechryd into your home to help you. Eventually, though, it was apparent that both of you needed outside assistance. That's when you and Aunty Pat decided to sell all your belongings, move to a nursing home and contact this lawyer the one on trial here today—to put your legal affairs in order.

To help prepare for your move, your nieces Shirley and Enid came to help. They had wardrobe, linens, and pantry duty for a week. My mother, Nora, came from Texas and she and I spent three weeks with you. Mom had office duty and took care of all your personal correspondence. She read your letters out loud, wrote to your business contacts and friends and organized papers you wanted to keep.

I was given house clearance duties: arranging an auction for your furniture, donating Margaret's gorgeous toys to the local toy museum, clearing the garage, and whatever else needed doing. Over eighty large bags of memorabilia from your lives were thrown away—photographs of friends and relatives, gifts from loved ones—you were preparing to exit our world. You said you could take nothing and wanted nothing.

As Mom and I waved good-bye, Uncle Kai and his wife, Hilary, arrived. It was their job to accompany you and Aunty Pat to the nursing home and to help you settle in, in the last move of your lives.

When I returned three months later to visit you, I saw you and Aunty Pat sitting quietly and motionless in the room you shared. The reality of how your lives had changed hit me like a brick. What had happened to the "in-charge" women who, when I was a young girl, ruled the world? You had become tiny, vulnerable, very old ladies who needed constant care. It seemed that you had given away your determination and feistiness and had faded to almost nothing. You said that you were waiting to die—you were ready— but then your lawyer rode in on his white horse. And that's when this awful swindle started.

You and Aunty Pat looked forward to his visits. You couldn't wait to see him. He recited Tennyson and spoke to you in your native tongue. Whatever he said in Welsh made you laugh again. The fact that I had no idea of what you were talking about didn't matter a bit; whatever it was delighted you. Who would think that he had wormed his way into your heart for the sole purpose of embezzling your estate?

Several things you told me about his visits made me uncomfortable, and eventually I became suspicious. It was some time before I finally had proof that he was thieving. There was no telling how much he had stolen from Aunty Pat before she died.

When Aunty Pat passed away, Mom flew immediately to the UK. I picked her up at Heathrow (I was living in London then) and we drove to Bangor to be with you and attend Pat's funeral. Of course your "lawyer-like-a-son" was already with you to comfort you in your loss. I told Mom then that I feared he had stolen from Aunty Pat and was now targeting you. She tried to put my mind at ease, saying I had surely mistaken his good intentions.

Having been given your power of attorney I wrote to the British Bar Association to ask them to investigate. I heard nothing back. But a call from the Bangor police fraud squad asking for copies of any correspondence with your lawyer confirmed my worst suspicions; they had started their own investigation. I hired a reputable legal firm to look into it, and they found he was draining your bank accounts dry. Not only was your lawyer embezzling from your estate, but it appeared that he was also stealing from the estates of at least four other families at the same time!

Now, as this trial has progressed and the evidence has revealed just how much this conman schemed to rob a blind, deaf and crippled ninety-one-year-old lady, I believe we will win this case and he will go to jail.

Being battered for four days in court by men whom I have never met but who are dressed in wigs and black undertaker robes has been surreal, Aunty. Before I return to the courtroom, I need to know for sure that you want him to go to jail. Oh, please, Aunty, send me a sign, tell me I am doing the right thing!

Aunty Lou? Did you just push back the clouds to let the sun shine? Did you stop the rain? YES! Thank you, Aunty Lou!

Now, Aunty…let's go get the bastard! —*KGM*

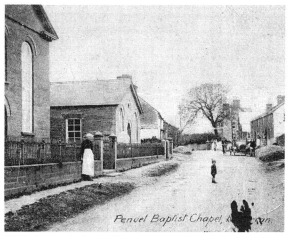

Willie Larsen in front of Penuel Baptist Chapel, Cilgerran, 1922

Willie's Story

Willie!

I suppose I attained my first degree of independence from the Griffiths family the moment my parents decided not to name me Moses. Moses was a traditional Griffiths name, but I wasn't a traditional boy. When my name was mentioned by anyone in our village it was always pronounced, emphatically, "Willie!"

If I had been born in today's world I would have been diagnosed with a condition called attention deficit disorder. But in the world of 1920's Cilgerran, I was considered to be a very, very naughty boy who was out of control, wouldn't concentrate on school work and needed strong discipline from the back of his mother's hand. No one knew about ADD then. Like many children with ADD, I had no sense of danger so I took no caution. It is a miracle I survived my childhood at all; I was always in trouble of some sort.

Unlike my mother, my father, Kai Larsen, found little wrong with my bad behavior. Dad, being a sensitive artistic type, admired my daring spirit, as his own dreams of adventure had died the moment he married my strong-willed mother. His lack of support for her strict discipline where I was concerned caused constant friction between them. Still, I was Dad's favorite and he saved me from her wrath more times than I could count.

It was difficult for Mum to defend my bad behavior to the disapproving villagers—the shaking of their heads and the "tsk, tsk, tsk" of Cilgerran tongues revealed their criticism of Mum's parenting skills and caused her deep humiliation. She defended me when they complained, but she bruised my bottom in private. Mum was terrified, she said, that I would end up dead like cousin Harold almost did.

My older teenage cousins, Harold and Ernie Thomas, lived near us in Cilgerran in a house called Kansas. They followed generations of village men into the quarries to work and they were my heroes. Sometimes, when I was a small lad, they'd let me go with them to their work at Dolbadau Quarry. Once Harold took me with him to the blasting room, where they kept the dynamite for blowing away the rock. It was my first time there and I felt very grown up by being included. The blasting room was off limits even to most of the quarrymen.

Somehow Harold managed to create a spark from a rock, which ignited the TNT. There was a huge blast. To my horror, the explosion blew off Harold's arm and took out one of his eyes. I could hardly speak while poor Harold lay bleeding on the blasting room floor.

Everyone in the village heard the explosion. As fast as they could get there, my grandfather, William, and Harold's mother, Aunty Margaret, ran to our aid. What a gruesome scene! No one knew if Harold would live or die. I felt terrified, just like I did when I had one of those horrible nightmares that made me wet my bed.

My grandfather picked me up and carried me home while I sobbed for Harold on his shoulder. It was whispered that my cousin would probably die from his injuries. My grandfather told my mother that I was not to be punished—for once it was not my fault. But just being there and being "Willie!" made me a prime suspect.

Harold survived, thankfully, and became a one-handed master slate cutter at my grandfather's quarry. He was a hero, see, just like I always knew!

The quarrymen in the pit operated huge brass and steel machines that cut and removed tons of rock. I dreamed of working in the quarry and operating one of them. But it would be years before I could do that, so I thought the next best thing to running a machine would be to take a ride on one. When I was about five years old and no one was watching, I climbed up the giant crane onto the enormous bucket filled with tons of slate. It would soon dump the rock onto the slag pile, and I thought it would be great fun to ride the bucket to the dumpsite. My plan was to hold on to its side so I wouldn't slide out with the slate.

Lucky for me, when the bucket was half way down to the slag dump I was spotted. One of the slaters waved his arms madly and screamed to shut down the machine. Soon all the men were yelling and waving. It was my first inkling that something was wrong.

Dolbadau Quarry steam crane (Tom Mathias)

The crane was stopped. The bucket and I were then lowered carefully to the ground. One of the men pulled me from the rocks and placed me safely into my grandfather's arms unharmed. A short time later, my mother's big hand found my small bottom.

I never forgot that spanking. Mum was afraid that I wouldn't remember the danger if I didn't feel the pain, so she hit me extra hard. I know now that she was trying to save me from myself, but the emotional scars of constantly being punished for being a bad boy never healed. Even as a young child I prepared for my escape, to free myself of my mother's strict rules.

The ancient walls of Cilgerran Castle provided a training ground for my future adventures. And its turret was my "boot camp." The turret was high and I could see the whole world from the top of those ruins. I even saw Africa and Tasmania, I imaged, the lands where I vowed to live as soon as I was old enough. The castle was a perfect place to practice courage under pressure and to hone the skills I would need to face the challenges and perils of my adult life.

When the other children were playing on the castle grounds, I often dragged my bicycle up the ancient walls to the old crumbling turret. Once on top, I reversed the seat so that it faced back to front and would ride my bicycle backwards around the turret—at least until one of the children would run to tell my mother.

Cilgerran Castle

Cousins Willie, Nesta, and Kai, in Cilgerran, 1936 (Tom Mathias)

No matter how much punishment my mother meted out, my bicycle and I returned again and again to the top of the world at Cilgerran Castle to prepare for escape. But I moved away earlier than I expected. And that turned out to be not such good thing after all.

By the time I was twelve or thirteen, my father had found work in Oxfordshire, so our family left Wales for England. In our idyllic country village of South Leigh, my mother's biggest fear came to pass: I was introduced to alcohol. Having a son who was fond of the bottle was painful beyond belief for Mum. My taste for alcohol started early, and at church no less! One Sunday the parson found himself a bell ringer short, so I volunteered to help, see. I soon became the permanent replacement and eventually had the distinction of being the only bell ringer who could ring four bells at once. That feat was accomplished by holding one bell in each hand and then putting my feet through loops I made and attached to the two other bell ropes. Fantastic fun! I was suspended in midair on the ropes, looking like a bell-ringing marionette. I could play Westminster Chimes in perfect timing. Well, sometimes.

To thank us for our hard work, the parson asked all the bell ringers to join him for lagers after Sunday services. He also helped himself to more than a few of those ales. One Sunday Mum smelled beer on my breath. She was furious and she let the parson know the depth of her rage in no uncertain terms. He, like any other person who walked on the wrong side of my mother's values, faced a tongue-lashing that surely was worse than death.

The parson probably never recovered from my mother's anger and I certainly never recovered from his poor judgment. Mum never forgave the man of God who handed me my first beer. I struggled with alcohol for the rest of my life.

Much of my life was spent trying to escape from my mother's strict values, but I carried her lessons with me all over the world, like a turtle that wears its house on its back. I could never escape, not even by moving thousands of miles away.

After the war I married a German girl whom I met behind enemy lines. Ursula was heroic in her own right and risked everything during the war to feed parentless children. She was as courageous a person as I had ever known, and she shared my dreams of adventure. We returned to Britain just long enough for me to finish my education and to acquire a teaching certificate.

We couldn't wait to discover lands unknown. I applied to the British Government for a teaching position in Kenya close to Nairobi and got the job. We moved as far away as we could get from a traditional life—first to Africa and then to Tasmania, the lands of my dreams.

We lead amazing adventurous lives. Often we faced a little more excitement than we had planned. In Africa we were captured and held in our home as prisoners for three days during the Mau Mau Rebellion of 1953. The Mau Mau "soldiers" were waiting for orders to execute us. We were British citizens. We devised a clever plan and escaped before being shot or hacked to death, like thirty-two other Brits who were living there at the time.

In the middle of the night, when the soldiers couldn't see us, we hung the loudspeakers from my ham radio set high in the trees surrounding our house. Then, in a prearranged plan, we called a friend on our ham radio, who, after introducing himself as God, spoke to the Mau Mau through the speakers from the trees. They couldn't see him, and it sounded just like God was speaking to them from the heavens.

God advised them that he was the Almighty and that they must set the British teachers free or he would kill them and their families. He would also see to it that they would spend a very painful eternity in hell.

The Mau Mau heard God loud and clear and they did exactly what he told them to do. They ran like *milgi*s, and we drove as far away as fast as we could!

Although I didn't realize it until I was older, I was very fortunate that my life was built on my mother's solid Welsh values. They held me fast and kept me true to myself when I encountered the unfamiliar on my life's journeys. And I was especially grateful to the ancient Welshman—no doubt someone named Moses—who helped build the turret at Cilgerran Castle. What my ancestors built saved my life in so many ways.

But I also know this: I, Willie!, would never have traded my free-spirited life for a traditional one! —*KGM*

Willie Larsen, c. 1940

Willie, Nora, and Kai, 1929

Kai's Story
A Need to Focus

My mother, Nora, named me Kay in honor of her beloved brother, Kai Larsen. I always hated my name, but when I finally met my gentle, handsome uncle, I changed my mind—then I felt as if it was a gift. Even though I knew that the only things we shared were our names and a connection through blood, I wanted to be just like him.

Uncle Kai saw beauty in everything—even ME! He told me that there were wonders everywhere and that the best way to see the things others couldn't see was through the magic of a lens. Everything, he said, held a secret inside. With a twist of the focus ring on his microscope or his camera, Uncle Kai became my tour guide though magnificent secret worlds.

Uncle Kai's need to "focus," my grandmother Sarah Mary told me, started when Kai was a little boy in Cilgerran. He was an easy baby to care for, but his brother, Willie, was hyperactive and needed her constant attention. Often, in order to get on with her housework, Sarah Mary placed both boys and their toys in a confined space where she knew they would be safe.

"Uncle Willie's mind would immediately escape to a place of freedom outside his confinement," she said. "But Kai was Willie's opposite. He found comfort and fascination in whatever was closest to him. Kai bloomed where he was planted."

It wasn't easy being the quiet, middle child; sometimes Kai felt he was invisible to his parents. Willie was the apple of his father's eye and the object of Sarah Mary's watchfulness. Little Nora was charming, outgoing and popular. Only at school was Kai a star. He excelled in everything.

Although his parents didn't have money for books to read for pleasure, Kai was able to fill the family bookcase with those he won in grammar school contests. Kai was proud of his contribution, and his collection was one of the few achievements that his father recognized.

Every summer the family traveled from their home in Oxfordshire to Cilgerran. How they got there was not easy. Kai's father drove a motorbike with a sidecar, which carried Sarah Mary and Nora. Kai and Willie rode their bicycles. At night, to save money, Nora and her parents slept at a B&B, while the two boys slept close by in a tent on the ground. Along the way, Kai would ponder the beauty of the countryside and slow down to study things that caught his eye, while Willie would pedal as fast as he could to get to the top of the next hill.

Kai's father could keep up easily with Willie on the motorbike, but Kai had to struggle. His father would tease him and sing "Have you ever seen a dream walking? Well, I have!"

When Kai's father praised Willie for being such a "man," the inference was that Kai wasn't. The bullying his father used, to try to make Kai more like Willie, only led to self-doubt in Kai's mind. Kai was probably the most capable child in the family, but he battled feelings of inadequacy for years.

Kai and Nesta on the Teifi, Cilgerran (Tom Mathias)

As a young boy, Kai set three goals for himself: to build a camera, a film developing lab and a microscope. Lenses for his camera and microscope would be the most expensive part of his dream, and he knew he could never afford them. So the first thing he bought with the little pocket money he had was piece of glass to grind into lenses. Kai ground for hours on end to make them perfect. Soon he was ready to build his camera.

Around that time, Britain had entered WWII, so the family home was fitted with blackout curtains. Whenever the sirens signaled for the village to turn out its lights and pull the curtains, Kai would take the opportunity to develop his films; his "lab" was the total darkness. In the morning his photos were ready to be dried, so he would hang them on the porch. Little did the poor boy know that his proudest accomplishment would create a nightmare for his family.

Kai read everything he could about building microscopes and soon figured out how to make one out of old bicycle handlebars. He managed to put together an excellent microscope and decided to enter it in a science fair in Oxford. Proudly, he snapped a photo of his invention with his homemade camera and—during another night of air raids—developed the picture, which he planned to attach to his entry form. He hung the photo on the porch to dry. His ambition? To win another book for the family bookshelf—and to gain his father's approval.

The next morning, after a night of sirens and blackouts, a neighbor came to call on Sarah Mary. As she reached for the doorknocker she saw that Kai had hung another of his photographs on the porch. She looked. This one was strange. She saw some sort of mechanical thing. She looked again. The photo showed an odd-looking piece of equipment with nothing else in the shot. Since there was no sense of scale it looked to her to be gigantic. It looked… it looked just like an anti-aircraft gun!

The neighbor put two and two together (or so she thought), ripped the picture from the front porch and rushed it to the authorities. They agreed with her. The thing did, indeed, look like some type of anti-aircraft gun. Soon several police officers arrived at Kai's home. As they burst into the house, Kai's father tried to comfort his terrified family. There was some mistake! But the police arrested Kai's father, who was still a Danish citizen, without hesitation. He was taken away and jailed—and investigated for spying!

Fortunately, Kai's father was a colonel in the Home Guard and was released once the other villagers vouched for his good name. The microscope? Kai destroyed it.

Later, Kai was called to action in WWII. Any doubts his father had placed in his head about his manhood were soon put aside. On D-Day, Kai and some other young recruits were shuttled to France in a glider to remove the wounded and give them medical aid. The young man sitting belted in on the seat beside him was scared to death—they all were. Bullets were flying at the glider, creating holes in the aircraft as they prepared to land. Kai asked the young soldier to his left if he was all right, but before the man could answer he slumped forward towards Kai. He had been shot in the head; he was dead.

When the glider landed, the medics found themselves in the middle of a raging battle and ran for the nearest cover. Kai jumped into a foxhole. When the air cleared enough to look around he found he was in a ditch that was littered with the bodies of dead German soldiers—except for one. He was wounded but alive. Kai took his bag from his back and went to work to save the man's life.

After a couple of days in their hell-hole, a group of German soldiers arrived to rescue any of their men left on the battlefield. The soldier whose life Kai had saved begged his comrades to spare his English friend. The German soldiers led Kai to an area where he could walk back across to the British line.

Although he was reported as "missing in action" for some time, Kai returned to Britain physically unharmed. After the war he married his sister's best friend, Hilary Forrest, had three children and taught science and botany at a school in Cornwall. He never really felt the need to travel back to Wales much. He spent most of his time in his beloved Cornish garden. Kai always bloomed where he was planted. —*KGM*

Nora hugs Kai, home from the war

105

William Griffiths of Llechryd, coracle maker (Tom Mathias)

Bernard Thomas's Story

Murder on the Teifi

I'm the last one, you know. After me there'll be no more old-time coracle makers left to tell you anything. So it was a good thing you noticed the coracles propped up along the fence in front of my house in Llechryd and stopped to ask me about them.

I know the real reason you came to see me was because you were looking for stories about your ancestors. Yanks, it seems, are always on a quest to find them. My old three-legged chow and I had all the time in the world to talk, and I was happy to help. I knew a few of your people, all right, and told you about them...and some more tales, too.

You'll remember, I know, the story of one of your relatives by the name of William Griffiths. This was the William Griffiths who lived in Llechryd, not the quarryman in Cilgerran who was your great-grandfather. William Griffiths of Llechryd was a coracle maker just like me. William Griffiths and my grandfather were connected, you see...by murder! It was because of the murder of my great-grandfather, the Teifi water bailiff.

William Griffiths lived along Lady Walk Lane in a house that was then called Brengast. He was a master coracle maker and soaked his willows in the stream in the back of his house by the well that they named Moses Well, after their oldest son, who died in his early twenties.

Now, I tell you, William Griffiths was an honorable and just man. When this story took place, times were very rough, and the people of Llechryd and Cilgerran were hungry and poor. They depended on fish from the Teifi to feed their families. But to fish for salmon in their own river, the people were forced to buy a license, see, which was really a tax on fishing. Very few could afford one. And anyway, it limited the number of fish that could be caught.

If the water bailiff caught anyone fishing on the Teifi without a license, he prosecuted him and there was a big price to pay, even imprisonment. But if the man who put fish on his family's table was imprisoned, his family could not survive. The villagers were trapped. There was nothing they could do but secretly poach food for their families—and hate the water bailiff.

One day, the water bailiff's son (my grandfather) shot his father dead with a hunting rifle in front of the water bailiff's home. The son swore it was an accident, but for some reason few people in the village believed him. The water bailiff, after all, was a devil of a man who jailed the poor and probably deserved to be shot!

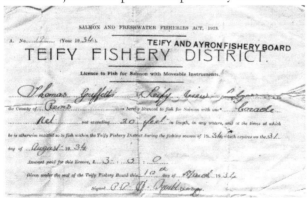

Tom Griffiths's 1934 fishing license

So a meeting was called and all the men of Llechryd gathered in a house, which still stands directly in front of the Llechryd Bridge. No women were allowed, of course. The village men took it upon themselves to decide the fate of my grandfather. If they found he was guilty, the sheriff would be summoned and the son would be turned over to the law and tried for murder. If he was found to be innocent, the shooting would be treated as a sad accident.

After the men listened to my grandfather's story of how he came to shoot his own father, a vote was taken. The outcome was almost unanimous: "not guilty," they all said—except for one man, William Griffiths of Brengast, coracle maker. He alone voted guilty.

William Griffiths was angry about the injustice of a "not guilty" vote and said to the men, "You all know this was no accident! Why are you voting not guilty? Is there no justice for a murdered man?"

One of the men responded as spokesman for the lot. "William!" he said. "The man was a water bailiff and we're all better off because his son did us this favor. The man shouldn't be punished for putting food on our tables!" The rest of the men were of the same opinion and said so, loud and clear.

So the murder of the Teifi's most despised man went unpunished for the greater good. And the villagers could bet that it would be some time before another water bailiff was brave enough to take the job! The fishermen rejoiced and, once again, untaxed fish graced the tables of the families of the Teifi.

I never held that guilty vote against William Griffiths, you know. He did what he thought was right and a brave man he was, to, to say what he did, even if he went against my grandfather. You can tell people I told you that story, see.

Oh, but wait: when you write it down, don't forget to say that I crossed the English Channel in a coracle that I built myself. It took me three tries, but I made it across and proved that if I could do it, so could thousands of Welshmen before me. There, now, I proved that, didn't I? And it was only thirteen and a half hours, it took me to cross!

*Teifi River near Llechryd Bridge, and the house on
the river bank where the "jury" met (Tom Mathias)*

And don't forget to tell the people that I was shipwrecked off
the coast of Africa in WWII and that the British Government
refused to give me back pay when they found out I had been
rescued and was alive, eleven months after being torpedoed. They
said shipwrecked sailors weren't entitled to back pay. And me, a
decorated sailor, a wounded sailor, being punished because I
survived. I hope that policy has changed by now. Bloody
outrageous, that was!

Today, not many people are left around here who remember
that I was a master coracle maker and an active servant of this
community. I want you to tell that I helped build the Cilgerran
Village Hall with another one of your relatives, Abram John
Griffiths. And don't forget to tell them all how beautiful and well
made my coracles were! There's even one in Manordeifi Church,
tell them.

Don't forget to tell them! —*KGM*

Kay and her prized investiture pillow, 2013

Kay's Story

It Takes a Village (or a Family)

Tales that my Welsh mother, grandmother, aunts and great aunts shared with me have shaped my character, moral code, politics and just about everything else about me. Their stories of the past, present and even the future have nurtured me like rain and sunshine nourish the soil.

My mother, Nora, sang and told stories until the day she died at age eighty-five. When I was a child she must have taught me every nursery rhyme that was ever written; I still know many of them by heart. The tales she chose to share with her children, even the hundreds of children that she knew during fifty-three years of teaching pre-school, were stories that would develop compassion and open-mindedness. As a dedicated educator, she carefully planned them that way. Each story had three consistent components: a lack of judgmentalism, a call for empathy and an abundance of tolerance. Because of the strong values my mother taught through her stories, I have come to love the word "liberal."

Reading was a struggle for me the first twelve years of my life. No one knew what dyslexia was in the 1950's, so listening to the stories my family told was the way I gathered information. Quietly, I would inch my way towards any sounds of adult conversations and eavesdrop on the stories they shared—until I got caught.

My grandmother Sarah Mary Griffiths told stories of the future. She saw it in the leaves at the bottoms of our empty teacups. If the tea leaves didn't clearly reveal our fortunes, however, she'd dump them into a saucer and discard them. The empty cup was placed upside down in the center of the dining room table amongst small bits of paper, each with a letter of the alphabet written on it.

The Mystical Spirit of the Teifi was then ceremoniously summoned by Grandma to help her decipher our destinies. Grandma would instruct the fortune seeker to place her index fingers lightly on the cup next to her own. After a long wait and lots of dramatic eye rolling by my grandmother, the Spirit would move the cup from one piece of paper to another. Letter by letter the stories of our futures were spelled out. None of us figured out that Grandma's fortune telling was a masterful technique—a "psych job"— that she used to stamp the blueprint she created for our lives into our subconscious. We accepted what she said without question. And, without fail, she was right. Grandma, you see, was a sorceress. She really was.

My great-aunt Martha Hannah Griffiths, known to my brother, sister, cousins and me as Aunty Pat, shared her love of history with me. As a child, I sat at her feet during summer evenings and basked in the tales of Gellert, King Arthur, Alfred the Great, Boudicca, Gruffydd and many other legendary heroes. She could recall every detail of their stories at will.

Sarah Mary reveals Nora's future

There were never enough tales of courage to satisfy. I dreamed of heroes every night after she finally sent me to bed. Aunty Pat brought the legends to life, and my friendship with them grew closer each time she retold their stories. Becoming so familiar with those legends put me, I believed, in an "inner circle of friends" of some of the greatest people who had ever lived. My love affair with history grew directly from tales she handed down.

Aunty Louisa, on the other hand, had no time for dwelling on stories of the past or conjuring up future ones like her sisters. She lived in the present. She made up her own tales as she traveled along life's path. And they were outrageous!

In 1969, when my brother, Stuart, and my mother and I were visiting her in Wales, Aunty Lou managed to get us all tickets to the investiture of the Prince of Wales at Caernarvon Castle. Our seats were far from the actual ceremony, but it didn't matter— we were there!

Only "toffs" and noblemen were allowed to sit in the royal enclosure. Those dignitaries had beautiful comfy orange pillows to sit on, with gold tassels and the Prince of Wales feathers carved on a large button in the center.

Aunty Lou decided that our family was "toff enough" to have pillows, too. So she marched her tiny frame up to the guard, gestured toward the royal seats and said, in the shrillest, poshest accent she could muster, "Excuse me, could you show us to our seats, please?"

The guard politely asked to see her invitation, whereupon Aunty replied with great aplomb and indignation, "Do you not know who I am?"

My mother looked as if she would die of embarrassment. I was holding back fits of laughter and my little brother was holding his breath at the thought that he might have one of those bright orange Prince of Wales cushions for his very own.

The poor guard was undone by Aunty Lou's tone and immediately showed us to our lovely orange cushions on the front row just a few feet from Queen Elizabeth's "throne." We had front row seats for the whole ceremony. I still have those cushions and will never part with them.

The storytellers in my life had very different personalities, but their tales of courage, charity and the human spirit carried the same message. I have leaned on their strengths and colorful tales to get me through life's crises. My story, without a doubt, is the sum of their stories as well as my own. —*KGM*

Sarah Mary, Kay, and Nora, 1949

114

Kay and her parents, Ronnie and Nora Garcia, in Mexico, c. 1954

Nora's Story

Escape to Mexico

Every summer my mother, Nora, yearned to trade the scorched grass and searing heat of Texas for the cool, green hills of West Wales. My father was a struggling law student at the University of Texas, so he wasn't able to afford that luxury. To comfort my homesick mother, Dad would drive us to the next best place and nearest mountain range—in the north of Mexico.

One particular trip to Mexico was made memorable by the fact that heavy storms had washed away the old bridge on the Rio Grande River just as we were preparing to cross the Texas border, into the land of my father's father. It was hard to believe how quickly flash-flood waters could appear out of nowhere. Other cars, buses and trucks that were in line to cross into Mexico were either immobilized or floating around freely, so we weren't able to move forward or backward. Soon the raging waters started swirling violently and pushed many of the cars into each other. Dad, a champion swimmer, opened the car window and crawled out into the muddy currents. Still in his twenties, he was too young to know how perilously close to death he might have been.

He rounded up some other men and they pow-wowed for a while before plucking a floating branch from the rapids. They cut notches into the wooden stick and plunged it to the ground below. It served as a gauge to check the rising water levels. If the stick showed that the water was rising, Dad's only option would be to lead his family, on foot through the dangerous waters, to higher ground.

Nora with Bonzo, Cilgerran, 1930

To keep me calm, although she was clearly fighting her own fear, my young Welsh mother, Nora, recited rhymes and insisted that I join in with her. For hours we sang, crayoned in a book, and made up knock-knock jokes. Looking out of the window I saw a dead dog float past me and burst into tears. Quick as a wink, Mom told the story of her favorite sheepdog who had died and gone to animal paradise when she was a little girl in Cilgerran. Soon I was happy for the lucky dead dog I'd seen in the flood waters because I knew he was bounding through lovely green fields with fire hydrants all over the place in animal paradise! Mom believed that to be a true story, she said, because the parson in Cilgerran had told her so.

Dad had told Mom and me to stay in the car as it was the safest place—the water hadn't risen past the car window. Our Ford station wagon was airtight, so we were quite comfortable, but the poor passengers in the Greyhound bus behind us had climbed onto its roof. There were children and old people all shivering in the rain. Distraught, I asked Mom to tell the stories of "The Little Match Girl,' who shivered in the cold like the people on the bus, and of the two children who fell in the River Teifi and drowned on their way to deliver eggs to their aunty in Llechryd. But she refused to tell those tales—they must have seemed a little too close to home.

After several hours, a very old, wrinkled lady waded up to our car window. The water was hip deep so wading was a struggle for her. Mom wanted the lady to get back on the bus in case she got washed away, but the lady didn't understand English and Mom didn't speak Spanish. Soon it became clear that she wanted food and water for her grandchildren.

"The language of desperation is universal," Mom told my Dad when he returned to our car. She assured him that we had packed more than enough food to share. Then she told me to pick out some of my favorite snacks to give to the old lady's grandchildren. NOT the ones I liked least, she said, but the ones I thought they would like most. Packages upon packages of chocolate Easter eggs, popcorn rabbits, sugar chicks, Spam, bread, tinned milk and potted meat had been packed into a large box which lay on the floorboard of the back seat of our car. I picked out my favorites (well, I did keep a few for myself) and handed a pillowcase full to the grateful woman.

It had become our family's tradition to have an Easter egg hunt on Saddle Mountain, outside Monterrey, Mexico, during our annual trip. Dad would divert my attention while Mom hid the Easter treats behind the coconut and date palms.

The fruit trees, Mom said, reminded her of Cilgerran where she, her cousin Nesta and other children loved to climb the apple trees. When Margaret Hannah Rees, who lived at the bottom of Dolbadau Road, walked past, Mom and Nesta would try to drop apples squarely on her poor head. "We were very naughty," Mom said, "but Margaret Hannah was kind enough to pretend that the apples we dropped surprised her and that didn't see us hiding in the trees."

Once the Easter treats were gathered up, Mom and Dad would drive to a tiny village with adobe huts and grass roofs so I could give away the Easter treats to the half-naked children who lived on the mountainside. Mom always gave them the clothes that children at her kindergarten had outgrown, and I was expected to sort out my clothes and toys to give them, too. The village children looked forward to our visits; our Easter holiday was like Christmas to them. Mexico was never wholly Mexico to me; it was always Wales in disguise.

When my mother grew old she longed for Mexico and the cool green mountains that reminded her of West Wales. In the end, I think she missed the mountains of Mexico as much as she missed the green hills of West Wales. —KGM

Nora with her dog, Cottonball, at her home in Austin, Texas, 2008

Parting Words from Nora
All Roads Lead to Wales

No matter where I traveled, I took Wales with me. I immersed my children in her stories, passed on to them her values and traditions, and took them to visit the land of my birth many times. Sometimes I thought they loved Wales even more than I did; they considered themselves equally Welsh and Texan, odd as that may sound.

Although I didn't retain much of my Welsh language as an adult, when I spoke to my own children I used the Welsh phrases that I used to hear in my childhood home. Four generations later, deep in the heart of Texas, I have heard my great-grandchildren use a strange blend of Welsh words intermingled with American dialect. I often laughed when I heard *ugh y fy* come from my Irish, American and Greek sons-in-law. Thanks to my mother, Sarah Mary Griffiths Larsen, and to the distress of my Aunts Pat and

119

Louisa (Griffiths), a few Welsh swear words also emigrated across the pond and landed in the mouths of my children.

My Danish father, Kai Larsen, once told me proudly that our very Welsh Griffiths family had Viking blood flowing through their veins. It was entirely possible, he said, to be Welsh and to be Viking at the same time, according to the books he had studied. He had determined that the Vikings crossed the Irish Channel and raided Pembrokeshire on a regular basis. "Once they got to Cilgerran," he said, "they fell in love with the landscape and the ladies, too—so in Cilgerran they stayed, just like I did!" The people of Cilgerran, he assured me, were Vikings even though they didn't know it. And that would explain a lot!

The Griffiths family's hearts have always been stretched between home and afar. Many of us were filled with wanderlust and became world travelers, while others of us immigrated to other countries. Leaving Wales didn't mean that we didn't love her—Wales was always home. It just meant that we were following our dreams to wherever they would lead.

Everything, it seems, has come full circle. Now that my own children and my cousin Nesta's children are adults, their dreams lead them back to Wales, as often as they can get there. I am so very pleased that they return, but what makes me happiest is that they travel back to Wales together, as a family.

I hope we have passed on the importance of keeping our families alive through our stories, so that our children and their children and grandchildren will know more about how they became who they are. Stories make people immortal—and families, too.

My Aunt Pat would often tell me, "Welsh blood flows through our veins—it connects us. Remember who you are and where you came from. Remember for your own sake and for your children's sakes. Remember you are Welsh, but most of all, remember you are family."

Remember, remember! —*KGM*

Griffiths-Mathias Families of Cilgerran, Pembrokeshire, Wales

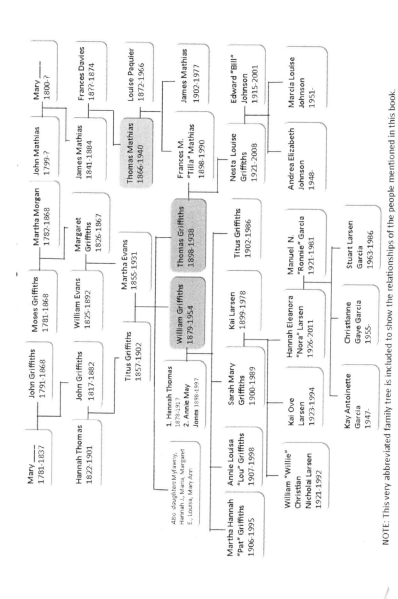

NOTE: This very abbreviated family tree is included to show the relationships of the people mentioned in this book.